D1605804

Political Religions

by
Erich Voegelin

translated by
T.J. DiNapoli
and
E.S. Easterly III

Toronto Studies in Theology
Volume 23

The Edwin Mellen Press

BV
631
.V613
1985

Library of Congress Cataloging-in-Publication Data

Voegelin, Erich, 1901-
   Political religions.

   (Toronto studies in theology ; v. 23)
   Translation of: Die politischen Religionen.
   1. Church and state. 2. Religion. I. Title. II. Series.
BV631.V613 1985   291.1'77   85-28524
ISBN 0-88946-767-6 (alk. paper)

This is volume 23 in the continuing series
Toronto Studies in Theology
Volume 23 ISBN 0-88946-767-6
TSR Series ISBN 0-88946-975-X

The Edwin Mellen Press
Box 450
Lewiston, New York
USA   14092

Printed in the United States of America

CONTENTS

INTRODUCTION

Eric Voegelin was born in Cologne, January 3, 1901, the son of Otto Stefan Voegelin, a civil engineer, and Elizabeth Ruehl Voegelin. In 1910 the family removed to Vienna, where Eric Voegelin resided until he was forced to flee to Switzerland following the occupation of the country by the Nazis in 1938. He left because he was on a Nazi hit-list; he attained that honourable position chiefly as a result of his writing four books during the 1930s, the last and most polemical of which was *The Political Religions.*

His secondary education in Vienna stressed modern languages, mathematics and science. In 1917, for example, he studied Einstein's new theory of relativity with his high-school teacher. Following the excitement of the Bolshevik Revolution, Voegelin read Marx's *Capital* and, until he studied first-year economics with Ludwig von Mises, considered himself a Marxist. In later life he was fond of saying that after he learned a little economics, Marxism ceased to be a problem.

When he entered the University of Vienna, his interests were drawn to mathematics, to law, and to the new program in political science. He eventually chose the last because, he said, his enthusiasm for mathematics had waned and he was equally unexcited about the prospect of becoming a civil servant, which is what a law degree almost certainly would have meant. In addition, a political science degree could be earned in three years rather than the more usual four, a significant consideration owing to Voegelin's poverty. He completed his doctorate with Hans Kelsen and Othmar Spann in 1922. Kelsen was famous for having drafted the post-war Austrian constitution and as author of the "pure theory of law." Voegelin later introduced Kelsen's doctrine to the United States.[1] Spann introduced Voegelin to the study of classical political philosophy and to the modern system-builders, Fichte, Hegel, and Schelling.

According to his long-time friend, Gregor Sebba, Vienna during their student days, a "shabby, sardonically cheerful city was an invigorating cultural center of the first order, teeming with talent, ideas, experiments, hospitable to every kind of intellectual venture from the stiffly orthodox to the wayward." It was still possible, Sebba said, "to bring together scholars and politically engaged people of every persuasion for informal debate on the burning current issues —probably the last group where Liberal and Marxist, Jew and antisemite, Socialist and Monarchist sat down together until civil war ended all that in 1934."[2] The civil disturbances of 1934, as Voegelin later argued, made necessary the establishment of an "authoritarian state" as an attempt to protect Austrian society against ideological sectarian political movements. During this period Voegelin participated fully in the intellectual life of the city, attending the private seminars of Kelsen, Spann and von Mises, as well as the less formal *Geistkreis* to which Sebba referred. This group met monthly to discuss a wide range of topics.

The appeal of Hans Kelsen for Voegelin lay in his analytical precision. Kelsen's drafting of the constitution, his court decisions, and his commentary on the constitution taught Voegelin the necessity of a careful and responsible reading of texts. The logical coherence of the legal system was supplied by the pure theory of law. In principle, Voegelin has maintained that double vision, of logical coherence and of careful and responsible fedility to texts, throughout his own philosophical work. His disagreement with Kelsen came not over the theory of law but over the commitment by Kelsen to a neo-Kantian methodology that attempted to delimit the field of study by the method used in its explanation. This was a methodological shortcoming that Voegelin detected in much more obvious ways with Marxism, racist thinking, scientism, and any number of other ideological movements. Eventually, Voegelin disagreed with Kelsen over just this methodological point. Kelsen believed that the logic of the legal system defined the field of study of politics generally. Under pressure of events in 1934, Voegelin realized that political problems were more comprehensive than legal ones; that the law, as Madison wrote in *The Federalist*, Number 48, was but a parchment barrier in the absence of a genuine political community. As early as 1924, Voegelin published an essay contrasting the pure theory of law with the wider range of materials covered by the study of politics as practiced during the early nineteenth century.[3]

Othmar Spann was a more comprehensive scholar than was Kelsen. His importance for Voegelin's later life is twofold: first, he introduced Voegelin to the problems of classical philosophy. But second, and in some ways more significantly, Spann's romantic nationalsim attracted a circle of romantically nationalist students. These people were important in a negative way, for some of them later became involved in the Nazi movement and in even more radical political movements opposed to the Nazis. During the mid and late 1930's Voegelin saw first-hand, in his former associates, the consequences of intellectual irrationality applied directly to political activism.

In 1922 Voegelin obtained a fellowship to attend summer school in Oxford. Officially he was there to improve his English. In addition, however, he was able to attend the lectures of Gilbert Murray, the distinguished British classicist. For a brilliant young man of twenty-one years, a summer in Oxford at the feet of Murray held the promise of expanding his intellectual horizons through contact with a civilized foreign culture.

Two years later he won an even greater opportunity for study, a Laura Spellman Rockefeller Fellowship, which took him to the United States for two years work at Columbia, Harvard, and Wisconsin. The importance of this first stay in the United States lay in the fact that Voegelin was forced to confront directly the larger world that lay beyond central Europe as well as the day-to-day problems of living in a vigorous democracy. Equally important, he escaped the recondite intellectual disputes of Vienna. Under the tutelage of John Dewey and Erwin Edman, Voegelin discovered English commonsense philosophy, eventually reading the works of Hamilton and Reid.

Very briefly, the British commonsense philosophers argued that commonsense was an attitude towards reality that was equivalent to the attitude of the philosopher, but without the linguistic and technical apparatus used by the philosophers to express their attitude. The other side of the commonsense philosophers' teaching was that philosophy, chiefly classical and stoic philosophy, was an analytically elaborate articulation of the commonsense attitude or experience. In his later works, this insight regarding the relationship of attitude and sentiment regarding reality, what he later called reality experienced, became a central pillar of his interpretative enterprise. The first conclusion that Voegelin drew, however, was political. The continued tradition of the experiences, sentiments, attitudes and insights of classical philosophy without the complicated discursive trappings of sophisticated academic language meant a great deal for the intellectual climate of opinion and for the cohesion and public

decency of a society. The example of America was
before him. Conversely, Voegelin recognized that the
highly erudite and abstract language of German
philosophy and German social science was empty of
commonsense. The philosophical form remained, but
the substance of the philosophical attitude towards the
great political questions of justice and injustice,
moderation and immoderation, piety and impiety, was
absent. This had, and still has, great and disastrous
consequences for public decency in Germany. The
difference between contemporary Germany and the
Germany of sixty years ago, Voegelin has said, lies in
the comparatively low intellectual stature of the
contemporary positivists, neo-Hegelians, existentialists,
Marxists and what-not who carry on these enthusiastic
debates.

The first lesson he drew from his stay in the United
States was that substantively American society enacted
or lived out a philosophical tradition more
comprehensive and meaningful than anything he had
discovered in Europe. American pragmatism, as this
commonsense attitude has been called, was less
articulate than the methodological environment of
Germany, but by the same token, that is what enabled
Americans to retain their sense of the concrete.
Voegelin was impressed, for example, with Dewey's
category of "Likemindedness," a term used in the King
James translation of the Bible to render the Greek term
homonoia. And *homonoia* was a problem in classical

and Christian philosophy about which a great deal had been written. Voegelin realized that Dewey was, in effect, working on the same problem, the problem of spiritual community, that classical and Christian thinkers had considered. This impressed him powerfully as evidence of the real or substantive continuity of the Western spiritual tradition in the United States.

The following year Voegelin left New York for Cambridge and Harvard. There he encountered Alfred North Whitehead, newly arrived from Cambridge, England. The second term of 1925-26 was spent at Wisconsin where Voegelin met John R. Commons, whose *Human Nature and Property* had been published the year before. Commons introduced Voegelin to the major themes of American government, especially the Supreme Court. A final Anglo-American influence on Voegelin during his stay in the United States was George Santayana, whom he studied at the suggestion of Erwin Edman. Santayana's scepticism was the perfect complement to the commonsense of Dewey and the metaphysical questioning of Whitehead. Santayana was immensely learned, like Voegelin's European teachers, but completely uninterested in the dogmatic squabbles of neo-Kantians.

In 1928 Voegelin's first book, *On the Form of the American Spirit*, appeared. The five chapters reflected the several topics he studied during his stay. The first, on time and existence, synthesized his studies of English and Scottish commonsense, Hodgson's philosophy of consciousness, the speculations of James and Peirce on time, contingency, and "radical empiricism." Implicit, and sometimes explicit, was a comparison of these Anglo-American thinkers with the German theory of "internal time-consciousness" represented by the phenomenology of Husserl. A second chapter was devoted to Santayana; the third to Puritan mysticism, chiefly represented by Jonathan Edwards. Chapter Four, some fifty pages in length, was concerned with the Anglo-American analytical theory of law. The two parts, on British and American variations in the theory of law, was compared to the pure theory of Kelsen. A final chapter was on John R. Commons.

The book is important both for understanding the intellectual development of Voegelin and as one of several accounts of America written by foreigners. We would like to emphasize its first aspect. For two years Voegelin was living in an environment where the level of sheer intelligence and brain-power was equal to that he had known in Vienna, but the concerns of the people he met had nothing at all to do with the heretofore important questions of methodological polemic. Instead of considering the merits of the Marburg versus the Southwest German School of neo-Kantians, Americans were concerned with the act of political foundation and the implications of the American founding through the political and legal culture represented by the founding fathers, by Lincoln, by the decisions of the Supreme Court. The background of

Christianity and classical culture as a living reality informed the discussion of the great American political institutions. None of this was present in Europe. What Voegelin discovered, upon reflection, was that there could be, as William James indicated, a plurality of worlds. Consciousness of plurality, and specifically of the difference in substance and in form between the highly articulate intellectual culture of central Europe and the substantive commonsense of America was captured in the closing words of Voegelin's book, in a quotation from Commons:

> I do not see why there is not as much idealism of its kind in breeding a perfect animal or a Wisconsin No. 7 ear of corn, or in devising an absolutely exact instrument for measuring a thousand cubic feet of gas, or for measuring exactly the amount of butter or casein in milk, as there is in chipping out a Venus de Milo or erecting a Parthenon.... Of course, a cow is just a cow, and can never become a Winged Victory. But within her field of human endeavour she is capable of approaching an ideal. And, more than that, she is an ideal that every farmer and farmer's boy —the despised slaves and helots of Greece— can aspire to.[4]

The immediate effect of his exposure to America was that Voegelin was innoculated from the intellectual and ideological extravagance that attended such events as the publication of Heidegger's famous book, *Being and Time*. Voegelin's priorities had changed: what was most important was reality experienced, not the debates derived or removed from reality, to say nothing of debates whose relationship to reality was tenuous or non-existent. The longer term effect was that this insight concerning plurality was transformed into an interpretative strategy: the plurality of lived experiences express the plurality of human possibilities, which in turn are realized in a plurality of political forms and civiliations.

The third year of his fellowship allowed Voegelin to study in France. As with his time in the United States, Voegelin was again immersed in the real-live problems of cultural and intellectual pluralism. He read widely among the symbolist poets and Valery; he worked his way through the great literature of the eighteenth and nineteenth centuries, discovering on the way that the French history of consciousness runs parallel in some respects with the English and American. Bergson's great work, *The Two Sources of Morality and Religion* was not yet published, though Voegelin read his earlier studies. In addition he was attracted to French memoirs, a genre that began in the seventeenth century. Finally, Voegelin plunged into the literature of the French moralists. It is probably fair to say that his time in Paris resulted in less dramatic changes than did his time in the United States. One insight, at least, was reinforced: the study of literature, and especially of poetry, is a kind of self-articulation of language. Voegelin's French studies emphasized again the importance of self-interpretation in the study of meaning. Throughout his writing, Voegelin has consistently maintained that one must retain a strict fidelity to what in 1928 he called "self-speaking phenomena," and what later were termed symbolisms. One does so by paying close attention to meanings as they are understood from the inside or imaginatively. The shock of America and Voegelin's response to it, his overcoming of central European provincialism without succumbing to American provincialism, brought this home to him in everyday life. It was confirmed by his reading the culturally more familiar French writers.

The experience of America awakened in Voegelin an awareness of the limitations of the central European intellectual culture that had nourished him. At the same time it enabled him to understand the greatness of those who devoted their lives to resisting what he later called ideological swindles. Among these scholars was Max Weber. Weber had a lasting influence on Voegelin in three areas. First, Weber's long essays of 1904-5 on Marx and Marxism destroyed whatever pretention to science that Marxists ever claimed. Weber's analysis showed, very simply, that Marx's writing was untenable ideology. Weber taught a more radical criticism than the implicit rejection of Marxism that the study of economics entailed. Second, Weber's distinction between the "ethics of intention" and the "ethics of responsibility" contained the genuine and permanent insight that the unforseen consequences of moralistic action are the responsibility of the actor. This insight, which could be formulated in commonsensical terms as well, was important because it was developed in opposition to the ideological position that if one cherishes certain "values" with great conviction, the "sincerity" with which they are held and the morally elevated intentions that one makes public are sufficient to excuse any suffering that might be caused by trying to put them into action. Weber's distinction made it clear that the "values" that are assumed to be so morally elevating are not only not scientifically valid, they are ideological inventions. It was for this reason that Weber developed his famous "value-free" method of inquiry devoted to the analysis of cause-and-effect relations in the process of society. The great defect with this method of analysis, as Voegelin pointed out later in *The New Science of Politics*, was that the criteria by which materials were accumulated for analysis as well as the reasons for an ethics of responsibility were themselves identified as "value-judgements" and thereby outside the boundaries of scientific or rational analysis. What saved Weber from relativism was, apparently, his personal mysticism: Weber experienced reality though he was unable to account for it. So far as science was concerned this was not entirely satisfactory; after all, students and other readers wish to know the reasons why an ethics of responsibility, for example, is superior to an ethics of intention. Moreover, when the rational order of existence is excluded in principle, passions are likely to move you to embrace the high moralism of elevated ends in which considerations of means are eclipsed; this is a recipe for ideological fanaticism.

The third area in which Max Weber, among others, was a model for Voegelin, was in the range of his scholarship. With his usual bluntness, Voegelin remarked that Weber established once and for all that one cannot be a successful scholar in the field of social and political science unless one knows what one is talking about. In this regard Weber, with his knowledge not only of modern civilization but of ancient and medieval civilization, of Near Eastern and Far Eastern civilization, and of India, remains an inspiration. Without this command of the empirical materials, Voegelin said, one cannot call oneself a scientist or comparativist.

In addition to Weber, the great classical scholar Eduard Meyer and the circle around Stefan George produced works during the late 1920s and 1930s that served to shape the intellectual climate influencing Voegelin. And finally, the literary influence of Karl Kraus should be mentioned. For ten years before his death in 1937, Kraus defended the Language of Goethe against the corruption of the journalists, the publicists, and the extraordinary vulgarity of the politicians. His equivalent in English would be someone such as George Orwell or Richard Weaver. As with Weber's insistence on comparative knowledge for an empirical scientist, Kraus and George taught that restoring shape and dignity to Language meant a recovery of the subject matter expressed by language, a recovery of meaning. A concern with language is part of the resistance against ideological nonsense inasmuch as ideologies seek to destroy not language but the consciousness of reality expressed through language, and to substitute for it a derived language expressive of the alienation from reality by the ideologue.

From the foregoing remarks it is clear that by the early 1930s Eric Voegelin was a superbly trained young scholar. Not only had he undertaken the usual academic exercises, but he had travelled widely and, more importantly, his travels had actually had the effect that travel is supposed to have: it broadened his understanding rather than confirmed his prejudices. His experience in America had innoculated him forever against the temptations of high-sounding abstractions just as Weber's ethical teaching had taught him the importance of political responsibility, prudence, and the importance of consequences for judging the justice of political action. In the language of classical philosophy, his psyche was well ordered. The times, however, were anything but well ordered. Voegelin's four books of the 1930s were all concerned with the political catastrophe that was about to occur, or rather, that had already begun and was to engulf the world within a few years.

The Bolshevik revolution was undertaken by men who said they were Marxists. The interpretative principle that instructs the political philosopher to begin with the self-interpretation of individuals and of events indicated that the work of Marx would be central to a serious understanding of the new Bolshevik regime, a regime whose most obvious characteristic was the practice of large scale, state directed murder. The study of Marx and of the first regime inspired by Marx's teaching ensured that the general problem of ideology would be a central topic of analysis. The second political event that sharpened Voegelin's concern with ideology was the rise of Fascism and National Socialism. These were collective political disasters, not personal tragedies or regrettable errors; the appropriate attitude of a political scientist under such circumstances was to resist the growth of these ideologies through an analysis of the fraudulent language and constricted experience of their practitioners. Voegelin undertook this resistance the way philosophers do, by careful analysis, by exegesis, and judgement.

In 1933, the year Adolf Hitler became chancellor of the German Reich, Voegelin published two books on race, *Race and State* and *The History of the Race Idea*. The first book analyses the pretentions of the "race idea" to scientific legitimacy. It does so by submitting the biological, anthropolological and ethnographic claims of this "idea" to analysis and systematic exposition. In a sense, by undertaking a "scientific" study of the claims to science of this "idea" Voegelin was conducting a magnificent parody. Many readers of this book have wondered how Voegelin was able to maintain his detachment, *sine ira et studio*. In part, Voegelin may have wanted to fool the Nazi censors; it is more likely, however, that he followed the procedure indicated earlier. If the race "theorists" consider their doctrine to be science, then, he may have said, Let us compare it with the findings of biology. When it is found not to accord with biological science, let us account for this error in methodological terms, as a "mistake" in the "primodial manner of seeing." A careful reader of the introduction to this study, where concepts such as "primordial manner of seeing" were introduced, would soon discover that Veogelin was, in fact, concerned with spiritual disorder. The background to Voegelin's understanding of biology was acquired during his stay at Columbia where he became friends with a number of young biologists, including Kurt Stern who was at work on genetics theory using the famous fruit fly. As Max Weber taught, he knew what he was talking about.

The second book, *The History of the Race Idea*, was one of Voegelin's best. It began with the words: "The knowledge of man has come to grief," and went on to explain that evidence for this grief was to be found in the current state of "race theory" as "inauthentic thinking." The key to the inauthenticity of thought, more fundamental than the deformations of scientific biology, was the denial of the Greek and Christian conception of human existence as a unity of body and soul. Accordingly, no scientistic reduction of human existence to its genetic or other immanent or material constituents could achieve anything but the destruction of social and political order. Voegelin undertook a lengthy critical analysis of the genealogy of the race "idea" and showed its convergence with other ideological systems, notably liberalism and Marxism. In any event, the Nazi race "theories" rested not upon experience, since there was no biological or ethnological basis for the notion of race, but upon dogmatic superstition that Voegelin identified with a perversion of natural science. Coupled to scientistic superstitions was a twisted millenarianism that transformed the Germans into salvific carriers of the Nordic Idea, and Jews into the diabolical "anti-idea." The combination of scientism and millenarianism had the logical implication that the triumph of the Nordic Idea required the physical extermination of the bearers of the material that constituted the Jewish "anti-idea." Here was a recipe for mass murder.

In March 1933, the Austrian government declared that Parliament had eliminated itself and that a new "authoritarian" regime had established itself. Three years later Voegelin published a book analyzing the new regime. The first part of the book is an analysis of the terms "total" and "authoritarian." These terms

were not theoretical concepts but political symbols that
served to express the assumption of a collective entity
ruled by a state institution that was itself governed by
whomever happened to represent the collectivity. The
second part of the book surveyed the problem of
constitutionality in Austria since the establishment of
the Dual Monarchy in 1848. What makes this material
currently topical is the argument that modern nations
and states are not "totalities" ruled by "authoritarian"
regimes. The existence of a body politic is a complex
reality based on a large number of impermanent ethnic,
ideological, economic, religious, historical etc. factors.
When new regimes are created, as was the Austrian
regime of 1933, by revolutionary fiat, their viability
will depend not upon the legality of the foundation,
since they establish new legal foundations, but upon
the degree to which they are able to create a stable
political body through the experience of participation
in a genuine political community. It was apparently
Voegelin's view that the "authoritarian state," with all
its shortcomings as a political body, nevertheless was
able to defend Austria against the ideological
radicalism of left and right. It might serve, therefore as
a chrysalis within which a political community might
develop. In the event, the annexation of Austria by the
Nazis and the inaction by the Western powers put an
end to these expectations. In the third part of the book
Voegelin made a detailed analysis of Kelsen's "pure
theory" of law and its connection to Austrian politics.

Or rather, he showed that Kelsen's legal theory was inadequate to the properly scientific understanding of political reality.

The last of Voegelin's four books written in response to the political crisis of the 1930's was the one produced here for the first time in nearly half a century, *The Political Religions*. It appeared in the spring of 1938 just in time to be confiscated by the invading Nazis. As with his postwar use of the term "gnosticism," Voegelin later expressed reservations over his use of the term "religion" to describe an ideological movement. The terminology was not simply wrong so much as vague and undiscriminating. The great change between this book and its predecessors, which may well reflect both the growing intensity of the political crisis and the awareness by Voegelin of the depth of the disaster that was about to break, is the increasing sharpness of his rhetoric. Ideologies now appear as spiritual diseases whose origins lay in the late Middle Ages when sectarian religious movements grew too powerful to be publicly suppressed as heresies. With the decapitation of God during the Enlightenment and His proclaimed murder during the nineteenth century, ersatz and immanent "political religions" were invented to express the deformed emotions and sentiments that once were expressed through Christian worship. In place of divine transfiguration through grace in death, humans sought to transfigure themselves into perfect men or supermen. The central argument of the book, which adequately expresses a fundamental truth, is that ideologies are by and large anti-Christian religious movements.

Certain subsidiary themes have lost none of their validity. The inadequacy of most critical analyses of ideological movements is a consequence of the dogmatic commitments of most contemporary intellectuals. The raising of questions of spirituality is rigorously excluded by positivists, Marxists, Freudians, and, of course, progressivist liberals. But if ideology is spiritual disease, their analyses are bound to be misleading. To state the question more aggressively, one might say that they are accomplices in their own destruction. If "metaphysics" has become a term of abuse and religious commitment an "illusion" whose future demise is to be anticipated with scientific satisfaction by psychoanalysts, one is not left with many insightful diagnostic instruments.

Despite the soberness of Voegelin's analysis, despite the implications contained in the epigraph, the first words above the gate to the Inferno, despite the lament of the Epilogue for the innocent about to perish, despite the failure of this book to comprehend the demonic evil of the age, despite, indeed, the human ability to flood the world with sufficient foulness to obscure the God who sustains it, men still cannot alter the structure of existence. When God is eclipsed by ideological dogma, the world supplies its own ersatz gods; when the symbols that express the human search for the divine source of justice and being are destroyed, world-immanent symbols that express human alienation from the divine ground are developed in their place. The analysis of the deformed symbols and the varieties of alienation, no less than the exegesis of symbols that express the plurality of ways by which the structure of existence is expressed and made articulate, were the twin tasks of the new science of politics that Voegelin developed after the war.

Voegelin did his greatest work in the United States. His multivolume history of political ideas, his most famous books, *The New Science of Politics*, and his *magnum opus, Order and History*, were all written in America. It was in America, moreover, that he found the initial spiritual difference that enabled him to begin his long and difficult task of restoring to political science its proper grandeur as a science of human experiences of order. The four books on ideology, written under the pressure of strenuous events, of which the last is presented here in English, constitute the necessary initial and negative moment, the exposure of the lie.

Barry Cooper
Political Science Department
University of Calgary

ENDNOTES

[1]Voegelin, "Kelsen's Pure Theory of Law," *Political Science Quarterly*, XLII (1927), 268-76.

[2]Sebba, "Prelude and Variations on the Theme of Eric Voegelin," in Ellis Sandoz, ed., *Eric Voegelin's Thought: A Critical Appraisal*, (Durham, Duke University Press, 1982), 7.

[3]"Reine Rechtslehere und Staatslehre," *Zeitschrift fuer Offentliches Recht*, IV: 1,2 (1924), 80-131

[4]Voegelin, *Ueber die Form des Amerikanischen Geistes*, (Tuebingen, Mohr, 1928), 237-8.

TRANSLATORS' PREFACE

I

Like all true works of art, literature, and philosophy Eric Voegelin's *Political Religions* may be viewed as a reflection, indeed, an inevitable product of the age in which it was written. Published originally in April 1938 in Vienna the treatise is difficult to imagine apart from the cataclysmic events taking place in Europe at that time.

It was a time dominated completely by the figure of Adolf Hitler, whose racist, supremacist ideology would plunge the entire world into the second major conflict of this century. Appearing as it did, then, on the eve of World War II, Eric Voegelin's work surely stands out as an eloquent and courageous "voice in the wilderness," bearing testimony to mankind's undaunted pursuit of enlightenment and good during even the darkest of times.

On January 30, 1933 Adolf Hitler was appointed chancellor of Germany. Almost immediately the new government began to take prohibitive measures against its opposition. As yet uncertain of their popular mandate the Nazis moved quickly to solidify national support for their extremist policies. When less than a month after Hitler's appointment fire broke out in the Reichstag or parliament, the Nazis capitalized on the opportunity by blaming the arson on Germany's Communist party. A Dutchman by the name of Marinus van der Lubbe was apprehended fleeing the burning Reichstag, arrested, and tried for the crime. The trial which lasted seven months concluded with van der Lubbe's conviction and subsequent execution.

Historians are in disagreement as to whether van der Lubbe acted alone or in conspiracy with Communist party members or whether in fact the Nazis themselves were behind the crime.

In the hectic days following the Reichstag fire the Nazis suppressed the leftwing press and carried out wholesale arrests of communist and socialist party leaders. The first concentration camps date from this period. A few protests by leading writers and intellectuals were heard. In February numerous writers resigned their membership in the prestigious Prussian Academy of Art and Literature, among them Alfred Döblin, Ricarda Huch, Georg Kaiser, Thomas Mann, Jakob Wassermann, and Franz Werfel. Others were expelled, leaving only such early enthusiasts of the regime as Gottfried Benn, Oskar Loerke, and Ina Seidel untouched by the mounting government pressures.

On March 5 Hitler asked for and received a strong vote of confidence from the German people in nationwide parliamentary elections. Less than two weeks later on the 15th of the month Joseph Goebbels, who was Hitler's minister of propaganda, issued the first directives to the press regarding their rights and duties. Soon such other public media as radio, film, and the theatre received similar directives.

On March 24 the German parliament empowered Hitler to enact laws on its behalf, the effect being to entrust carte blanche powers to a man bent on world domination. Germany's Jews were the first victims of the regime's policies. They would also become its most harshly persecuted. Throughout the month of April sanctions were imposed on Jewish shopkeepers, civil servants, and other professionals severely restricting their activities and curtailing their basic freedoms.

In literature and the arts censorship was becoming more and more common. On May 10, less than four months since Hitler's appointment to the chancellorship of Germany, the first of many public book burnings was staged in Berlin. Others followed in Bonn, Cologne, Frankfurt, Göttingen, Hamburg, Munich, and Nuremberg. Among those writers whose works were consigned to the flames were Lion Feuchtwanger, Sigmund Freud, Heinrich Heine, Heinrich Mann, Erich Maria Remarque, Kurt Tucholsky, and Arnold Zweig.

State control of the arts increased throughout the summer of 1933. On September 22 legislation was passed regulating the so-called *Reichskulturkammer* or state cultural chambers under the jurisdiction of Joseph Goebbels. In order to pursue one's profession an artist or writer had to belong to such chambers. Jews were excluded from membership as were outspoken critics of the regime.

To bypass such restrictions writers resorted to a variety of ploys. Some adopted pseudonyms, others simply changed their names for good. The famous philosopher and literary critic Theodore Adorno, for instance, wrote under the name of Hektor Rottweiler. The anecdote is told about the writer Günther Stern, who was told by a close acquaintance that his name sounded Jewish. "Change your name," he was advised, i.e., in German "Nennen Sie sich anders!" (literally "call yourself 'anders' or something else) and so Stern did indeed decide to call himself something else -- Günther Anders.[1] Jewish writers in particular were sought out, arrested, and sent to concentration camps. The expressionist poet and playwright Erich Mühsam was tortured and murdered by the Nazis, as was the promising young poetess Gertrude Kolmar.

A particularly tragic story is told about Carl von Ossietzky who was editor of the weekly journal *Die Weltbühne* from October 1927 until March 7, 1933. Arrested following his lecture entitled "Kultur und Barbarei" ("Culture and Barbarism") before the League for Human Rights, Ossietzky was sent first to the concentration camp at Sonnenburg, later transferred to the camp at Papenburg-Esterwegen. It was here, while he was still in prison for his political beliefs, that Ossietzky was awarded the Nobel Prize for Peace on November 23, 1936. Finally released through the intercession of the International Red Cross, Ossietzky succumbed to the maltreatment he had received at the hands of the Nazis and died within two years of his release, on May 4, 1938. His tragic fate epitomized the demise of all men of conscience in Germany at this time.

Two months earlier on March 11, 1938 German troops had marched into Austria. The German press, which had regarded Ossietzky's receipt of the Nobel Prize as a scandal now hailed the annexation of Austria. Events within Germany were proceeding in lockstep. Throughout the Third Reich during the last years of the decade even more repressive measures were being undertaken to outlaw Jews and silence opponents of the regime. In the realm of art and literature, a low point was reached on July 19, 1937 when the government staged an exhibition of so-called "degenerate art" ("Entartete Kunst") in Munich and other cities.

Within the country a resistance movement began to mobilize its forces, drawn from various segments of the population. In Munich opposition coalesced around the brother and sister team of Hans and Sophie Scholl, whose "Weisse Rose" ("White Rose") group of students distributed hundreds of anti-Nazi leaflets during the war years. On February 22, 1943 the Scholls were arrested, subjected to a mock trial, and executed.

Within the Foreign Office a group known as the "Rote Kapelle" ("Red Cell") organized around the figures of Harro Schulz-Boysen and Arvid and Mildred Harnack. In 1942 nearly a hundred members of the clandestine underground organization were identified by a captured Russian agent, forced to confess his knowledge of the group by the Gestapo. Half of the group's members were subsequently tracked down and executed.

Opposition formed in the military as well. Led by Graf Claus Schenk von Stauffenberg, civilians and members of the armed forces launched a plot on July 20, 1944 to assassinate Hitler and top advisors on his staff. The attempt failed and a majority of the conspirators were quickly apprehended and executed in this famous "officers' plot."

The dangers of remaining in Germany during the nightmare years were great. Faced as they were with an ever deteriorating situation within the country most writers, artists and intellectuals chose to flee Germany for more secure havens in exile abroad. While the exact number of emigres is impossible to ascertain, it is estimated that about 1800 writers alone were forced into exile, with another 4000 playwrights, actors, producers, stage designers, and members of the film industry joining them to swell the ranks of exiled literati to nearly 6000.

Among the most prominent writers were Walter Benjamin, Bertolt Brecht, Hermann Broch, Thomas and Heinrich Mann, Robert Musil, Erwin Piscator, Anna Seghers, Ernst Toller, and Franz Werfel. Some of Germany's greatest minds also found themselves forced to emigrate during the Third Reich: Erich Auerbach, Ernst

Auerbach, Ernst Cassirer, and Albert Einstein to name but a few.

The destinations of these emigres were first of all those countries with cultural and/or linguistic ties to the homeland: Switzerland, Holland, Czechoslovakia. Other countries followed quickly — and inevitably, as German troops threatened more and more of Europe: Spain, Portugal, France, the Soviet Union, Palestine, Latin America, and the United States.

In all these countries centers invariably sprang up to foster German culture in exile. Given such a mass exodus of artists and intellectuals Germany's devastating loss in the cultural sphere became in time the gain of every country in which emigres found refuge. Though never a cohesive group in the strictest sense, emigres nonetheless were drawn together in a common desire to keep the spirit of German culture alive during the nightmare years of their banishment. Enclaves of German culture sprang up spontaneously in every one of these countries. Newspapers and journals were published for a German readership in exile; clubs, cabarets, and theatres opened as forums for the presentation of anti-fascist exile works.

Some examples: In Prague, the birthplace of Kafka, Rilke, and Werfel political cabarets opened under such names as the "Bert Brecht Club," the "Thomas Mann Club," or "Studio 1934." The literary journals "Die neue Weltbühne" and "Neue deutsche Blätter" were founded. The city even became the home of German

publishing firms forced into exile, the famous Malik
Verlag of Wieland Herzefeld and John Heartfield being
just one well-known example.

Between 1933-1935 in Amsterdam Thomas Mann's
son Klaus, who has achieved a modicum of fame today
as the author of the novel *Mephisto*, published a
monthly journal entitled "Die Sammlung" ("The
Anthology") with the assistance of Andre Gide, Aldous
Huxley, and his uncle Heinrich Mann.

In Paris a league of German writers (*Schutzverband
deutscher Schriftsteller*) formed in the summer of 1933
to protect and represent the interests of German authors
abroad. On May 10, 1934, the first anniversary of the
infamous book burnings in their homeland, German
emigres in Paris opened a library to house works
banned in Germany. Initially called the "Library of the
Burned Book"(*Bibliothek des verbrannten Buches*) the
facility was later renamed the German Library of
Freedom (*Deutsche Freiheits-bibliothek*) housing
nearly 20,000 volumes. Between the 21st and the 25th of
June 1935, the "first international writers' congress for
the defense of culture" convened with authors from 37
countries represented.

It was also in Paris in the spring of 1938 that the first
complete bibliography of German exile literature was
published by the journal "Das Buch" under the title
"Fünf Jahre freies deutsches Buch" ("Five Years of Free
German Books"). Paris was also the point of origin for
what has been labeled "camouflaged literature," i.e.,

works designed to be smuggled into Germany under innocuous or deceptive titles. Bodo Uhse's *Die letzte Schlacht* (*The last battle*), for example, was published as a schoolbook edition of Schiller's classic *Wallensteins Lager* (*Wallenstein's Camp*).

Moscow attracted numerous German writers, particularly those with communist ties: Johannes R. Becher, Willi Bredel, Alfred Kurella. When Germany invaded the Soviet Union on June 22, 1941 most of these writers were forced once again to flee. Some went to the United States (Erwin Piscator), others to Mexico (Anna Seghers) or other distant lands.

Switzerland, because of its long tradition of neutrality, became a mecca for German exiles. In Zurich, Mann's daughter Erika opened a satirical cabaret calling itself "Die Pfeffermühle" ("The Peppermill"). The city's famous Schauspielhaus theatre under the direction of Oskar Wälterlin provided German playwrights with a valuable outlet for their work. It was on this stage, for example, that such famous plays as Brecht's *Galileo Galilei* and *Mutter Courage* (*Mother Courage*) were first performed.

At an international conference in Glasgow, Scotland in 1934 a new German chapter of PEN was approved to represent the interests of German authors in exile.

In the United States German colonies sprang up in Princeton, New Jersey (Hermann Broch, Albert Einstein, Thomas Mann) and in Los Angeles,

California or in Hollywood (Theodore Adorno, Bertolt Brecht, Hanns Eisler, Lion Feuchtwanger, Fritz Lang, Peter Lorre, Thomas and Heinrich Mann, Max Reinhardt, Arnold Schönberg, Bruno Walter, and Franz Werfel). Erwin Piscator settled in New York, where he helped found the New School of Social Research.

South of the border Mexico attracted such important writers as Alexander Abusch, Erich Arendt, Ludwig Renn, and Anna Seghers. A journal, edited by Abusch, appeared monthly under the title *Freies Deutschland* (Free Germany). The most important publishing firm operated by German emigres in Mexico was called "El libro libre" ("The free book") and opened in 1942 on the 9th anniversary of the book burnings in Germany.

It was in Scandinavia, however, specifically Stockholm, Sweden, that the story of Eric Voegelin and his *Political Religions* resumes. Until the Austrian *Anschluss* of 1938 Vienna had been a logical haven for many emigres, particularly given the large number of reputable publishing houses in the city and because Vienna had always been a major center for the arts in Europe.[2]

It was here in Vienna that the respected firm of Samuel Fischer, under the directorship of Dr. Gottfried Bermann Fischer had emigrated from its original headquarters in Berlin. By means of sensitive negotiations with the ministry of propaganda, the old S. Fischer Verlag was permitted to maintain one branch in Germany, under the direction of Peter Suhrkamp, and another branch abroad.

Bermann Fischer first sought approval to locate this foreign branch in Switzerland, but his request was denied by Swiss authorities. At the end of 1935 Fischer travelled to Vienna, where on July 15, 1936 he was finally able to announce the opening of the new Bermann Fischer Verlag. The firm immediately began publishing authors under contract to the old German based S. Fischer Verlag, who had been banned under the Nazis. A total of 780,000 works were thus permitted to appear in print, which might otherwise have been lost. The firm's branch in Germany meanwhile continued to operate, publishing works by "approved" authors.

As in the case of so many individuals threatened by the annexation of Austria in 1938, the Bermann Fischer Verlag too found it more prudent to move on, as it did in the night from March 13 to March 14, 1938. Fischer's destination this time was Stockholm, since once again a request to resettle in Switzerland was rejected.

Under an agreement with the Stockholm based firm of Albert Bonnier, Fischer moved his entire operation north. On June 21, 1938 a notice appeared in

Stockholm's "Dagens Nyheter" ("Daily News") announcing the founding of a German language firm in the city — the Bermann Fischer Verlag Stockholm.

Among the authors — and important works — to appear in the Bermann Fischer Verlag were: Thomas Mann: "Schopenhauer," *Lotte in Weimar, Der Zauberberg (The Magic Mountain), Joseph der Ernährer (Joseph the Provider), Doktor Faustus,* and "Deutschland und die Deutschen" ("Germany and the Germans"); Franz Werfel: *Das Lied der Bernadette (The Song of Bernadette), Der veruntreute Himmel (Embezzled Heaven),* and *Stern der Ungeborenen (Star of the Unborn)*; Stefan Zweig: *Die Welt von Gestern (The World of Yesterday),* and *Balzac;* Martin Gumpert's "Dunant," Ernst Cassirer's "Descartes," and *Die politischen Religionen (The Political Religions)* by Erich Voegelius (sic) were also destined to appear in the Bermann Fischer Verlag.

With the German invasion of Denmark and Norway in April 1940 Fischer made the difficult decision to flee Sweden. Like his countryman Bertolt Brecht, Fischer first set out for the Soviet Union, before sailing on to the United States. There through personal contacts with the publishers Alfred Harcourt and Fritz Landshoff, Fischer was able to open the L.B. Fischer Publishing Corporation in New York, with the idea of making works by German authors available in English to an American audience.

Thus the long saga of the Fischer Verlag came to a close. That of Eric Voegelin's *Political Religions*, however, was just beginning![3] First published in Vienna during April, 1938, entirely confiscated by the Gestapo, then republished by the Bermann Fischer Verlag Stockholm in 1939, *Die Politischen Religionen* (*Political Religions*) marked a transitional time in Voegelin's life as he was forced to flee his home in Austria and live in exile in the United States. (Indeed, the new preface to the 1939 edition bears the author's location as Massachusetts). But these tangible, external changes pale in comparison to the subtle shifts in Voegelin's thought as evidenced by *Political Religions*.

For Voegelin, *Political Religions* expresses the fruition of the early scholar's intellectual endeavor, and also gives birth to much of what would become his later life's work. This brilliant, somewhat emotional essay reflects the course of thought developed in his *Rasse und Staat* (*Race and the State*) and *Die Rassenidee in der Geistesgeschichte* (*The Race Idea in Intellectual History*), both published in 1933, and *Der Autoritäre Staat* (*The Authoritarian State*), published in 1936. In these earlier writings Voegelin critiques, with a devastating calm, the attempts of Nazi doctrine and Marxist materialism to explain the necessarily religious bases for political order in terms of either genetics or economics.

This earlier critique reaches full expression in *Political Religions*, in which Voegelin articulates the principles, explains the processes, and identifies the root causes of political disorder from the cosmological empire of Ikhnaton in ancient Egypt to the then current heresies of Marxism and Nazism. Voegelin conjectured that such political disorder largely resulted from the secular effort to sever human existence from transcendental engendering experiences. This idea, which anticipates much of the scholarship of the later Voegelin, represents the maturing of the young Voegelin's thought.

Political Religions, unlike the measured scholarship of Voegelin's previous books, conveys an emotional quality in its rhetoric. It views the rejection of the transcendental as the source of order in political society and history (what Voegelin sometimes expresses metaphorically as the "decapitation of God"), as the ideological basis for the Marxist, Nazi and Fascist excesses occuring in Europe during the 1930s. This process of rejection explains much of the essentially religious character of these radically secularized political movements. Inherent in this rejection is the distinction between "spiritual" religions which partake of the divine BEYOND, and "political" religions which locate the divine within the contents of the world. The portended results of this distinction, and the processes involved, prompted Voegelin's passionate refutation of the political religions prevalent at that time.

Although never using the characterization of "gnostic", *Political Religions* embraces the essentials of the concept which dominates so much of Voegelin's later work. While it is not our purpose to critically review Voegelinian thought, an example seems appropriate to our purposes, i.e., his treatment of "apocalyptic" symbolism as expressed in political ideology. Perhaps, reflecting Voegelin's extensive, serious study of the writings of St. Thomas Aquinas and various Augustinian Jesuits, from about 1933 to 1935, *Political Religions* identifies parallels and correlations between the Christian conception of man's perfection at the end of history and the belief in the perfectability of man's reason as expressed in various ideological forms from the Enlightenment to the modern dynamic movements of Marxism and Nazism. In the gnostic eschatology, history becomes a sequence of ages, usually three, moving toward some ultimate fulfillment, each age is introduced by some "Leader" and posited by some "Prophet" (i.e., the modern "intellectual"), and gives rise to some future realm of perfection (i.e., the millennium). The expression of these symbols as means of self-interpretation in political society is at the root of what Voegelin later describes as gnosticism. However, this very expression receives Voegelin's attention throughout *Political Religions*.

Of course, Voegelin's later work was considerably more refined and his ideas concerning political religions much more developed than at the time of this essay's original publication. Even so, much of value is to be found on its pages. In the words of the later Voegelin: "The contemporary disorder will appear in a rather new light when we leave the 'climate of opinion' and, adopting the perspective of the historical sciences, acknowledge the problems of modernity to be caused by the predominance of Gnostic, Hermetic, and Alchemistic conceits, as well as by the Magic of violence as the means of transforming reality."[4]

II

In our translation of Erich Voegelin's *The Political Religions*, we were guided by the principle of "faithfulness to the original text," realizing that language is unique not only to the author, but also to the cultural community for which his work is intended. Furthermore, we recognize the fact that there is a world of difference between the mere communication of ideas and the personal manner in which these ideas are expressed.

In the case of Prof. Voegelin, the style is often as profound, as inimitable, as are the ideas for which it is the vehicle. This "valedictory of the young Voegelin," it must be remembered, was written at a time when the world about him succumbed to the seduction of "political religions" with long lineages—a matter very much at the fore of his thoughts. This presence of mind finds much expression in his *rhetoric*! As translators, then, we have tried to remain faithful not only to Prof. Voegelin's ideas, but to his *style* of writing as well. In all cases, however, we have been careful to keep in mind that our primary readers are not German, but rather English speakers, whose language adheres to different norms than does that of the language in which the original text is written.

In making the transition from German to English, we have often relied on Prof. Voegelin's own later writings in English—both for the rendering of specific concepts ("world immanent" for example), as well as for certain stylistic peculiarities. This is the case, for instance, in the English version of some of the Egyptian hymns quoted, which occur again in his work, *Israel and Revelation*.

We have also chosen to leave a number of German terms in the original language for several reasons. In some cases, the words in question are readily familiar to readers of historical, philosophical, or political tracts from the German: *Reich, Fuhrer, Volk, Angst*. Furthermore, it is also clear that such words are able to express a reality difficult to render in any other language, precisely because of their unique association with the German culture.

This is also true in other cases, where Prof. Voegelin has resorted to various neologisms to convey ideas incapable of being expressed adequately enough by existing terminology. Since such newly created words as "Realissimum" are as novel to German readers as to American, their translation would not only open the way for misinterpretation, but would also destroy to a certain extent the unique flavor of Prof. Voegelin's language.

Finally, there was the metaphoric nature of language itself to take into account. On occasion, Prof. Voegelin intentionally prefers one term to its otherwise legitimate synonym, precisely because of its metaphoric value. In all cases, however, we have tried to maintain a critical balance between language and idea, in the belief that it is only in this way that a translation will truly remain faithful to the original text and to its author.

T. J. Di Napoli
E. S. Easterly III

ENDNOTES

[1]Quoted in the Frankfurter Neue Presse, March 17, 1971.

[2]For an in-depth account of Vienna as an intellectual and cultural center see Allan Janik and Stephen Taulmin, *Wittgenstein's Vienna.* New York: Simon & Schuster, 1973 and Frederic Morton, *A Nervous Splendor. Vienna 1888/1889.* London: Weidenfeld & Nicholson, 1979.

[3]For a detailed discussion of the Bermann Fischer Verlag see Ludwig Hoffmann et al, *Exil in der Tschechoslowakei, in Grossbritannien, Skandinavien und Palästina.* Leipzig: Verlag Philipp Reclam, 1980, pp. 440-449, 692.

[4]Eric Voegelin, "Response to Professor Altizer's 'A New History and a New but Ancient God?'" *Journal of the American Academy of Religion,* XLIII, p. 769.

PREFACE

This treatise on political religions was published for the first time in April 1938, in Vienna. National Socialist publishers did little for its distribution with the result that the treatise has remained almost unknown. It has become well enough known, however, to find among discerning readers just as critical a reception as my earlier writings. My presentation has been accused of being so objective that it actually calls attention to those views of the world and these movements, in particular National Socialism, that it was intended to combat. What is missing is the decisiveness of judgment and evaluation that would place my own position beyond all doubt.

These critics touch upon fundamental questions concerning the present world situation and on the relation of the individual to it. There is a type of political intellectual today—and for the most part these critics belong to this type—who announces his deep abhorrence of National Socialism in vehement, ethical judgements; he regards it as his task and duty to lead the struggle with all the literary means at his disposal. *I* can do this too. My aversion to every sort of political collectivism is obvious—to anyone who can read—from the quotation by Dante that precedes this treatise; and my store of cultured and less cultured critical

expressions is manifest. That I do not express them
before a wider audience in the form of politicising
outpourings against National Socialism 7 has its
reasons. There are many reasons. I can touch upon only
a single, very essential one.

The political collective is not just a political and
moral phenomenon. The religious element in it seems
to me to be much more significant. The literary
struggle as an ethical aversion to propaganda is
important, but it becomes suspect when it conceals
what is essential. Doubly suspect: for it draws attention
away from that deeper and more dangerous evil that
lurks behind ethically disreputable acts; and, if it finds
no deeper basis than a moral code, it becomes
ineffective and questionable as far as its own means are
concerned. I do not want to say, however, that the
struggle against National Socialism should not also be
waged as an ethical one. It is simply not being
conducted radically enough, in my opinion, because
the radix, i.e., the root in religious experience, is
missing.

A religious view of National Socialism must proceed
from the assumption that there is evil in the world. To
be sure, evil not only as a deficient mode of Being,
something negative, but rather as a genuine, effective
substance and force in the world. A not merely
morally bad, but also a religiously evil, Satanic
substance can only be opposed by an equally strong,
religiously good force of resistance. A Satanic force

cannot be combated with morality and humanism alone.

This difficulty, however, cannot be alleviated by a simple decision. There is no significant thinker in the world today who does not know—and who has not expressed it—that the world finds itself in a severe crisis, in a process of decay that has its origin in the secularization of the spirit and in the separation of a therefore merely worldly spirit from its roots in religious experience; and who does not know that the remedy can only be arrived at through religious renewal, be it within the framework of traditional churches or outside of this framework. This renewal proceeds to a large extent only from great religious personalities; but it is possible for everyone to be prepared and to do his share to prepare the soil from which the resistance against evil will rise. [8]

On this point, however, politicising intellectuals fail completely. It is always dreadful to hear that National Socialism is a regression to barbarism, to the Dark Ages, to the times before the more recent advances towards humanism, without the speaker's sensing that the secularisation of life, which the concept of humanism brought with it, is precisely the soil in which anti-Christian religious movements such as National Socialism could grow. The religious question is taboo for these secularizing minds. And to pose it seriously and radically seems suspect to them—perhaps even a barbarism and a return to the Dark Ages.

It seems more important to me, therefore, to voice the basic religious questions of our time and to describe the phenomenon of evil that should be combated, than to involve myself in that ethical struggle of resistance. If my presentation awakens the impression that it is too "objective," and "campaigns" for National Socialism, then it seems to me that this is a sign that the presentation is a good one—for the Luciferian is not just a moral negative, a horror, but rather a force and indeed a very attractive force. The presentation would be bad if it called forth the impression that it only had to do with a morally insignificant, stupid, barbaric, despicable matter. The fact that I do not regard the force of evil as a force of good is evident from this treatise to anyone who is not insensitive to religious questions.

Cambridge, Mass.   Christmas, 1938 [9]

I

THE PROBLEM

To speak of political religions and to interpret the movements of our time not only as political, but above all as religious ones as well, is today far from self-evident, even though the evidence should compel the aware observer to this conclusion. The reason for this hesitancy lies in the use of symbolic language, which has taken hold in the last few centuries with the dissolution of western empires and with the coming into existence of the modern world of states. Whoever speaks about religion thinks of the institution of the Church; and whoever speaks about politics thinks of the State. These organizations are juxtaposed as clear, stable unities and the spirits that fill these bodies are of dissimilar natures. The State and the worldly spirit won their sphere of influence in a bitter struggle against the Holy Roman Empire of the Middle Ages; and in this conflict linguistic symbols were formed that do not recognize reality as such, but rather retain and seek to defend the antithesis of the struggle.

Concepts of the religious and the political have followed their institutions and their symbols. They have entered the field of battle and placed themselves under the authority of the conflicting linguistic

symbols, so that today, under the weight of their means
of conception, distinctions can still be recognized.
Perhaps through critical probing, however, at least
some instances can be found of the effectiveness of
closely related basic human forces. The concepts ⑪ of
Religion and the State, as they are related today in
general European lexical usage, as well as at the core of
the more restricted usage of science, orient themselves
in terms of definite models that have their specific
significance in the European intellectual struggle. By
religion, one understands such phenomena as
Christianity and the other great redemptive religions.
By the State, one understands the political organizations
on the order of the modern Nation-State. In order to
comprehend political religions adequately, we must
therefore enlarge the concept of the religious so that not
only redemptive religions are included, but also those
other phenomena that we recognize as religious in the
development of the State; and we must test the concept
of the State against it, to see if the State refers to nothing
other than secular, human relationships of organization
that have no connection to the religious sphere.

THE STATE

A textbook definition, which no one has suspected
until now of making religious claims, says that the
State is a federated union of settled people, endowed
with primal ruling power. A few elements of this

definition apparently refer to experiential evidence: people in a union, settled in an area. Another element, however, that of the primal ruling power, awakens doubt. "Primal" can signify simply that the power has no source other than the State itself and that it is derived from nowhere else, that it is absolute. A glance at reality shows this assertion to be false. An absolute, primal power is a power above all powers; it has no power beside or above it and lower powers exist only by its grace. The power of the ruler, however, [12] has internal bounds, because there are things that no ruler can do without being deposed; and it has external bounds imposed by other ruling powers.

A plurality of powers compels a further question as to their origin: the primal nature of power, its supremacy, has as its content a superlative—the assertion that the power in question is the highest. For Dante, it is self-evident that the plurality of powers would necessitate the question of their legitimacy and order; the question requires finding a formula for the unity among the myriad powers and, for the ordering of power with the transfer to the Supreme Power of the divine principles of unity. We notice nothing of such a duty in our textbook definition. Supremacy is asserted solely on the basis of an empirical judgment, plus a claim to accuracy. The completely articulated, created order is thereby decapitated; the divine head is struck off, and, in place of the world-transcendent God, the State appears as both the ultimate condition and the source of its own being. Unless we deny ourselves this rationalistic step and remain standing at this point, the mutually restrictive myriad forces put forth the thought of an all-encompassing unity and the belief that the world is populated by demonic forces, all equally primal; and that the question of unity is meaningless. The assertion of primality turns us away from the path of ordered thought; it sets us above the rules of reasonable inspection of empirical matters; it rejects rational discourse; the mind that conceives it changes from a partner in the discussion into a *Faktum* of another order, the origins of which we must pursue.

The textbook definition leaves us, to be sure, in the lurch, and we can only grope along as we ascend to the historic sources from which this assertion has sprung. It was Hegel who proposed the theory that the *Volk* as
13 the State was the spirit in its immediate reality and therefore the absolute power on earth. His forceful intellect does not stumble over details; he draws firm conclusions. If the State is absolutely powerful, then it may not have any internal bounds. The mechanical aspects of order and duty therefore belong to it, as do total obedience, the renunciation of personal opinion and debate, the denial of a personal spirit, and, at the same time, the intensive presence of the spirit, which resides in the State. The courage of the individual in the State is not personal, but rather mechanical, not that of a particular person, but rather that of a member of the whole. The mechanical means of killing were therefore

invented not by accident, but rather by the spirit that has become the State, in order to transform the personal form of courage into the impersonal. This homicidal urge is directed against an abstract foe, not against a person.

We can now sense more clearly just what stakes are involved. It does not have to do with the accuracy of a definition. It has to do with life and death. Still further, it has to do with the question of whether a human being may exist as an individual person or whether he must dissolve in an impersonal *Realissimum*. The contact between one human being and another is interrupted; non-human ideologies stand opposed, and man is transformed into a cog in a machine, playing along mechanically in the bustle of life, outwardly warring and killing abstractly. That the power of the State is primal, or absolute, is no longer a judgement of the person who submits to the State, but rather the dogma of a believer. Through this experience, the existence of man loses reality; the State appropriates it and becomes what is truly real and that from which a stream of reality flows back into men, transforming them with new vitality into parts of the suprahuman reality. We have entered the center of a religious experience, and our words describe a mystical process. [14]

The *Volksgeister*, which manifest themselves in states, have a definite relationship to one another and with the *Weltgeist*. As steps towards its realization in history, the states relate to the *Weltgeist* as human

beings relate to the State whose cogs they are. The rise
and fall of states in history is the verdict of that spirit,
and before it, every national spirit is condemned to
death when its earthly hour is finished. It is not blind
fate that rules over the states' struggle for power, rather
it is "World Reason" that displays itself therein. The
fates of nations as they are experienced by those who are
themselves actors in the historic process of the world
are just as meaningless before the decree of reason as the
fates of human beings are before the absolute power of
the State. Human beings are swallowed up by the
Realissimum of the State; before the *Realissimum* of
the *Weltgeist*, people and State disappear into the
impersonal nothingness of their instrumentality. The
question will always remain as to what is more
astonishing at this point of Hegelian speculation: the
imperative, world-ordering intellect that forces
historical matter into the revelation of the spirit or the
lack of sensitivity to the serious problem of theodicy if
the world spirit has no other means for realizing its goal
than with the blood and tears of humanity. The
gigantic structure of the strictly ordered system spans
an abyss of human nihilism, consuming itself in a
search for fulfillment of reality through a collective.

RELIGION

Man experiences his existence as a creature and
therefore as doubtful. Somewhere in the depths, at the
umbilicus of the soul, there where it touches the

cosmos, it strains. This is the place of those [15] stimuli which are inadequately referred to as "feelings" and which are therefore easily confused with similarly named, superficial movements of the soul. It is not easy to grasp their nature. Religiously motivated people describe them in images that only touch upon those features, and that they recognize in their own stimuli. They speak of primal feeling in order to indicate the depth of a "feeling" that is deeper in life's essence than other feelings. From this point they see the whole of existence. They speak of the infinity of feeling in order to say that it is not directed towards definite objects, but is basically a directionless, agitated surge. They call it a feeling of absolute dependence in order to depict their experience of the bond to a suprapersonal, almighty Something. They speak of being-thrown-into-life and of "abandonment," when the stimuli of an existence, once sheltered in the womb and now expelled, predominate. They come together from the *distentio*, the dispersion of their being, and return to the point of their origin in order to rediscover in the act of *intentio*, i.e., the reversion to God, themselves and Him. This experience of reunification can intensify to luminous phenomena of the divine. All the stimuli that arise out of the human condition of having been created can be colored differently, according to mood, as dread, hope, despair, piety, apparent calm, searching restlessness, outrage, rebellion, renunciation, and so forth.

The wealth of shadings that we have attempted to
indicate unfolds in a single dimension of religious
experience: in the stimuli of "having been created." It
is multiplied by the multifaceted nature of Being in
which the stimuli are fulfilled and satisfied. In all
directions in which human existence is open to the
world, the surrounding Beyond can be sought and
found in the body and in the spirit, in the individual
and in [16] society, in nature and in God. The great
number of basic possibilities that open up combine
with the attempts at self-interpretation, with all of
their misconceptions and distortions, to form an
inexhaustible store of experiences, rationalizations,
and system structures. For some, the doors of one's
existence stand wide open for a glimpse beyond the
steps of Being, from inanimate nature to God. The
world unfolds for them; the things of this world enter
into an orderly relationship with one another; they
combine with each other into an order of Being; they
combine with the system of values on the steps of Being
into an order of rank; and in answer to the question of
the reason for Being into an order of creation. A
maximum reception of reality combines with the
maximum of rationality in the order and union and is
crowned by the dogmatic re-formation of the spiritual-
religious experience in a divine idea, such as the West
has developed in the *analogia entis*. Others are granted
only scant glimpses of reality, perhaps only one: of
nature, a great person, his *Volk*, humanity. What is

seen becomes for him the *Realissimum*, the meta-reality; it takes the place of God and therefore conceals from him all else, even—and above all—God.

We have presented the question of complications arising from basic religious experiences so critically, by way of the types of *Realia* introduced, that the difficulties of recognition, which we pointed out in the introduction, become clear. Wherever something real is revealed in religious experience as something holy, it becomes the most real thing there is, the *Realissimum*. This essential re-orientation from the natural to the divine results in a sacred and value-oriented recrystallization of reality around that which is recognized as divine. Worlds of symbols, linguistic signs, and concepts arrange themselves around the divine center, [17] coalesce into systems, become imbued with the spirit of religious stimulation, and become fanatically defended as the "right" order of Being. Our age is filled to overflowing with religious orders of this type. The result is a Babylonian confusion of languages because the signs of a language have sharply different sacred, magical, and value connotations according to the speaker who is using them. Language within a *Volk* today is no longer generally binding, but rather torn into special languages along the lines of politico-religious splits. We lack the self-evident words with which the spiritual facts of this sphere might be named. Adherents of movements that claim to be anti-religious and atheistic resist the idea that at the foundation of their fanatical stances, religious experiences are to be found that revere as a religion something different from what they oppose. We must therefore make a linguistic decision: The spiritual religions, which find the *Realissimum* in the *Weltgrund*, should be termed for us "world-transcendent religions;" all others, which locate the divine in partial things of the world, should be called "world-immanent religions."

Let us now turn from the *Realia*, from the instances of Being in which the divine is recognized, and from the recrystallizations of reality around the *Realissimum*, back to the man who searches and finds. New varieties of perspicacity and breadth of vision, of accentuations of the will and feelings, of spirituality and instinctiveness reveal themselves. If the heart is sensitive and the intellect keen, then a glance at the world will suffice to see the misery of creatures and to sense the paths to salvation; if they are insensitive and dull, then massive impressions are necessary to draw out the weak feelings. The sheltered prince's son saw for the first time a beggar, an invalid, and a dead man—and became the Buddha. A modern writer [18] sees the mounds of corpses and the horrible destruction of thousands in the chaos of postwar Russia; it occurs to him that the world is not in order, and he writes a series of modest novels. The one sees in suffering the nature of creation and searches for salvation in the *Weltgrund*; the other sees it as an evil condition, that can and should be actively countered. Some souls address the inadequacy of the world more strongly; some deny the existential magnificence of creation. The one experiences a Beyond as real only when it is accompanied by splendor and bustle, by force and terror of a superior power in the form of a sovereign person and organization; for the other, the visage and demeanor of each person are transparent and allow his divine solitude to shine through. And the realms of the soul extend over a wide area from which ecstasies arise, experiences in which man transcends his existence: from the *unio mystica* of the spirit to the elevation in the communal festival, to the devotion to the brotherhood, to the loving reaching out of oneself into the landscape, to the plants and the animals, and on to the instinctive convulsions in the sexual act and in the intoxication of blood.

II

AKHENATON

The oldest political religion of a culturally advanced people was the sun worship of the Egyptians. Its beginnings flow back to the dawn of history, but its development, as we are familiar with it up to its apex in the sun cult of Akhenaton and the ensuing catastrophe, permits the outlines of the problem to be recognized more clearly than in the case of the later and better [19] known examples of the Mediterranean and European cultural sphere.

The particular factors in the course of development in which the myth unfolds are provided at the beginning of recorded time. The kings of the first dynasties already regard themselves as the successors of the sun god Horus, one of the rulers of the divine dynasty that ruled the country in its mythical beginning. The proto-dynastic kings of the still separate empires of the North and South, constituting the "Servants of Horus," enter into the ranks of demi-gods and are later venerated as gods in the cities where they ruled. The first historic kings, as the successors of Horus, bear his name as their favorite title and along with it the title of "a good god." After their deaths, they too are venerated in their temples as gods. Even the form of state religion already exists at the beginning of recorded time. The king is the mediator between man and the gods. He alone, theoretically, has the right to worship the gods; but practically speaking, he is represented as mediator in the various temples by high priests and religious cults.

Even the main figures of the inner politico-religious struggle for power are thus presented. There are countless local deities, whose spheres of power are not always clearly demarcated. Rather than simply one sun god, there are several of them in each of the large cities. Each god has his ministry, and the cults struggle among themselves to increase the stature of their god so that he is regarded as the highest. The decisive point in the struggle is the recognition by the god's intermediary, the king. Each of the priestly cults must therefore strive to acquire such a strong influence over the king that their god will emerge as the closest to the pharaoh, i.e., as the "State god."

In the transition from the Fourth to the Fifth Dynasty (ca. [20] 2750 B.C.), the struggle of the cults was decidedly in favor of the sun god of Heliopolis, Re. Several kings' names of the Fourth Dynasty already contain a reference to Re; in the transition to the Fifth Dynasty, the priests have become supporters of the king and determiners of kingship. The first king of the Fifth Dynasty was probably a high priest of Re, while the office of Wesir was exercised by a priest of Ptah. The State theology was further transformed: the king became the natural son of Re, and Re appeared on earth each time to become the father of the king. The official name of the king regularly contained the name of Re, and, from the end of the Fifth Dynasty, the title "Son of Re" appeared alongside the old title of Horus. The Horus of Edfu was supplanted, and the cult of Re became the State cult. The political upheaval, which is at the same time a religious one, is reflected in the revision of divine myths. Old myths are transformed and new ones emerge. Re, who had once ruled the empire as an earthly king with Toth as Wesir, becomes the king of Upper and Lower Egypt. From then on, the State theology conforms closely to political developments.

A further phase in the course of development is completed following the period of internal chaos that separates the Old Kingdom from the Middle Kingdom, at the time of the Twelfth Dynasty (2000-1788). The cult of Re survived the centuries, and its status rose so much that many sects interpreted their own particular god as a variant of Re in order to partake of his fame. The political focal point shifted from Memphis in the North to Thebes in the South. For this reason, the god of the new imperial capital, Amon of Thebes, who had formerly been an insignificant local deity, was transformed into Amon-Re in order to do justice to the new political meaning. Running parallel to the renewal of political unity was the [21] unification of the

one sun god. A further step on the road to the formation
of the monotheistic myth was accomplished.

After the time of Hyksos, in the New Kingdom, the
State religion followed the newly created, strict
military organization. "The religious orders of the
various sees, which had previously been separate and
which had coexisted side by side, were combined into a
large central order that embraced the entire country.
The chief of the State temple at Thebes, the high priest
of Amon, stood at the head of this order, and his power
therefore increased far beyond that of his old rivals in
Heliopolis and Memphis." Amon of Thebes had
become, with the victory of the Theban royal house, the
supreme god of the State. The queen became the spouse
of the god, and the wife of the Priest of Amon became
his first concubine.

The new military state advanced beyond the
boundaries of the old Upper and Lower Egyptian
kingdoms, and Egypt became a world empire. With
territorial expansion, the knowledge of new lands and
peoples, the influx of booty in gold and slaves, the new
luxuries and the flourishing of art, and with the new
overall political standing as a world power that enjoyed
a vigorous commerce with the Asiatic and Mediterranean
powers, the State religion also changed. "The myths
which conceived of the gods as kings who ruled the Nile
Valley originated when the story-tellers lived under
such kings. So now the priests of the New Kingdom,
now living under kings who ruled a world empire,

imagined in conceptual form a world domain and a
world plan as prerequisites for the idea of a world god."
The religious orders of all the greater gods began to
imbue the myths of their gods with cosmological and
demiurgic speculations, but generally in such a way
that the bounds of reality 22 of the god coincided with
the land of the Nile. Only in the case of the sun god did
the speculation go further. Under Amenothep III (1405-
1370), an old name for the sun, "Aton," was already
more frequently used in place of the name of the sun
god. The new use of the old name becomes significant
and completes the work that had begun with the
consolidation of the sun gods as manifestations of the
one Re in the middle Kingdom: Amenothep IV
introduced Aton as the supreme god. To be sure, he did
not dispute his identity with Re, but his intention went
beyond the cult of the sun as the visible god. Aton is not
the ray of sun, but rather "the glow that is in the sun";
Aton is the "Lord of the sun"; the new god is the life-
giving principle as such, as it reveals itself in the effect
of the sun. Amenothep had a new temple constructed
for him and thus the political debate began between the
new god and the old religious order, a debate which
ended with the removal not only of the old religious
orders, but also of the old gods. Their veneration ends
and their names are eradicated whenever found on
monuments. Even the name of the king's father,
Amenothep III, is obliterated from all the temples of
Thebes, because it contains the name of the god Amon.

Finally, the king changed his own name to Akhenaton, "It is pleasing to Aton." The task was completed when the king built in place of the old Theban city of Amon, three new cities to Aton, the new god of the empire, in the three parts of the empire—Egypt, Nubia, and Asia. The Egyptian city, Achet-Aton (later Tell-Amarna), became the residence of the king.

Aton assumed those functions of an imperial god which had originally been exercised by the old gods at the time when the world empire was expanding. The gods who originally ruled over the Nile Valley alone, themselves led [23] the troops of the king beyond the boundaries of the old country during the wars of conquest. The extension of the Egyptian boundary markers in Nubia and within Egypt simultaneously extended the possessions of the god. According to the State theology, the king conquered the world for god, and god's help was implored to increase the conquered world, i.e., god's domain. Because the king is a god himself, the divine and the human spheres merge. The empire conquered by man and the divinely created world, human and divine rule, human and divine creation, become difficult to distinguish.

From these preparatory beginnings, Akhenaton developed the idea of god with which we are familiar from his Aton-Hymns. Aton is through his luminosity the source of all life. He is the creator of man and of animals, of the earth and the Nile, of the seasons and their change. He crowns creation by revealing himself in the heart of Akhenaton. In the hymns, one can still recognize the origin of Aton in the deities of the Nile Valley. In the lines,

> The darkness is banished
> When Thou sendest forth Thy rays,
> Both lands celebrate daily a festival.

The two lands are Upper and Lower Egypt. On another occasion, the creation is elaborated upon:

> Thou didst create the world according to
>   Thy desire
> While Thou wert alone.
> The countries of Syria and Nubia,
> And the land of Egypt.

The created earth extends over the three parts of the empire, and Egypt is even mentioned last. Aton is a world god, his creative love and care 24 extend over all life, over the whole earth and all men without regard to race and language:

> Thou settest every man in his place
> Thou suppliest their necessities.
> Everyone has his food,
> And the time of his life is reckoned.
> Their tongues are diverse in speech,
> And their forms as well; their skins
>   are distinguished,
> As Thou distinguishest the foreign peoples.

The break with orthodox Egyptian tradition is very sharp: the king shows an unusual ability to free himself from the ties to a world that is identical to the land of the Nile and to embrace the breadth of the world as ordered creation in all of its variety. He was the first great religious individual in world history.

As remarkable as the wisdom and spirit of this single person is in his age, even he does not yet break with the Egyptian State religion. Aton is the one god, but he is no redeemer of mankind; he is the god of the Egyptian world empire; he cares for all in their existence, but he only descends to one, to the king, who speaks:

> Thou art in my heart,
> And there is no other that knows Thee,
> Save Thy son, Akenaton.

The old hierarchy of sacred substance is retained. Only through god's son is creation related to the creator from whom it sprang. Only a single individual in the world lives in an unmediated relationship to god: the mediator, the king. He alone knows the will of the lord:

[25]
> For Thou hast made him well-versed
>   in Thy plans;

and he is the bearer of the power that carries them out:

> For Thou hast made him well-versed
>   ...in Thy might.

A clear distinction is drawn between the ages of the world and the streams of power. Aton created the world out of his solitude:

> O sole god, like whom there is no other!
> Thou didst create the world according to
>   Thy desire,
> While Thou wert alone.

The creation continues beyond this first act, continuing as the eternal re-creation of the world in the daily course of the sun:

> The world is in Thy hand,
> Just as Thou hast made it.
> When Thou hast risen, then they
> (men) live;
> If Thou settest, then they die.
> For Thou Thyself art the time
> of life,
> And man liveth through Thee;
> All eyes behold Thy beauty,
> Until Thou setteth.

And with this, the circle closes. The stream of life, which flows over the world, generates not senseless life, but rather meaningful activity in service to Aton and his son:

> All work is laid aside
> When Thou setteth in the West.
> When Thou ariseth, it is done, [26]
> To grow for the king.
> Since Thou hath founded the earth,
> Thou hath established it for Thy son,
> Who procedeth from Thee Thyself.

The world and the empire are one, the son of god is the king, the stream of divine strength creates the world and further sustains it through the glow of the sun and the commands of the king who knows the divine will. And from below, the creation rises again in service to god.

In the reforms of Akhenaton, the sun myth reached the limits of its development. After the death of the king, there was a reaction and within a few generations a return to the veneration of the old gods. At the head of the reaction were the powerful leaders of the displaced religious cults and of the army, who had grimly watched the empire and its military power decline under the dominion of the reformer.

The restoration, however, had a broad basis because the people had been strongly agitated by the religious reform. This brings us to one last essential point in the creation of Akhenaton, the point at which the requirements and the limits of political religion become visible. We said that, with the establishment of the Aton cult, the old gods were set aside and their veneration interrupted. As far as it affected the previous State gods, this was above all of concern to the religious orders and the social classes that were close to the State's god. The culture of Egypt, however, was polytheistic. Alongside the State religion and its god, there were also apolitical gods and their cults. The most notable instance was that of Osiris, his cult, and his mystery plays. The Osiris and Death cults had joined together in an extensive complex of faith that dealt with the morality of earthly life, the judgement of the dead, life after death, and the punishment and rewards awaiting the individual soul 27 in the Beyond. It was the main religion of the lower classes. In the sacred hierarchy of the sun god, they were so far removed that the State religion could not have had any deep significance in their personal lives. Ontologically, the sun cult dealt with the problems of world and State, the Osiris cult with the fate of the individual soul. From a systematic, religious point of view, polytheism permitted the co-existence of religious spheres, without their having to come into conflict and without their having to be combined in one system for the sake of rational construction. Socially, the sun cult was closer to the governing classes; the Osiris cult to the governed. Through Akhenaton's reform, Osiris and his cult had been dismissed along with the other gods, thus delivering a severe blow to the religious life of Egypt, a life which had been socially balanced in polytheism. As for the political religion, only changes in personnel had taken place in the ruling class, and the monotheistic rationalization could have perhaps succeeded had the king in other respects been able to maintain the expansionist strength of the State. The religion of the people, however, had been destroyed in offering them the Aton cult as a possible substitute. The whole complex of religious life contained in the Osiris cult remained unsatisfied by the monotheistic imperial cult. The creative accomplishment of Akhenaton in the field of religion did not go beyond the development of the sun myth and did not contain elements of a personal ethic or a solution to the personal questions of life and death. With its hierarchy of sacred substance and the separation of the subjects'

lives from god, the pure State cult could only have
succeeded in a polytheistic system in which the other
essential elements of man could develop their own
religion alongside that of the political. [28]

III

We will sketch a few of the most important sacred symbols that helped achieve the union of the human-political sphere and the divine.

HIERARCHY

One basic form of legitimacy for the rule of man over man is realized in the symbol of radiation from a divine summit, through a hierarchy of rulers and offices, down to the last obedient subject. The symbol has a widely ramified history, and we will point out only a few of the forms that have become significant. We have already encountered this symbol at a very high degree of spiritualization in the sun myth of Akhenaton. In this regard the Egyptian development was not without consequences for later European development. It is certainly no accident that the symbols of the sun and of the emanation of divine substance have so decisive a place in the teachings of the Egyptian, Plotinus. The extent to which the natural cosmologic myth in the age of Ptolemy must have supplanted the spiritual one can once again be observed in the work on monarchy by Philo of Alexandria. He vigorously turns against the belief that the sun and the moon are sovereign gods and insists that the rulers are subordinate to an invisible

Logos in the performance of their offices. The symbol of a sacred outpouring was completely reformed by Maimonides (1135-1204), a man who so intensively assimilated all of eastern Mediterranean culture. From him the currents flow through multi-branched channels to western Europe.

A century after the Jewish philosopher had so painstakingly conceived the flowing-from-a-spring symbol at the Egyptian court, we encounter this [29] and the comparable symbol of light-emission in Dante's *Monarchia*: "Thus it is clear that the authority of secular monarchs has its immediate origin in the source of total authority without any sort of intercession. The Source, which exists in the utmost simplicity and unity, flows out of an immense goodness into many brooks;" the emperor, "illuminated by the paternal light of grace, is more strongly able to cast his rays upon the sphere of the earth." The symbol of the sun once again becomes the symbol of the monarch through Louis XIV (1638-1715). In his memoirs, he gives the reasons for the choice of this symbol in terms that remind us again of the hymn of Akhenaton: "Through its unique property, through the aura that surrounds it, through the light that it provides other stars, which form a sort of court around it, through the equal and just dispersal of light to the regions of the earth, through the good that it creates everywhere, insofar as it incessantly promotes life, joy, and activity everywhere, and through its untiring movement, in which, however, it always appears calm, through its continuous and unchanging course from which it never deviates or turns aside, the symbol of the sun is certainly the most vital and most beautiful for a great monarch."

At the end of the sixteenth century, Bodin, the great theorist of the French kingdom, elaborated the symbol of the sacred hierarchy down to its particulars in the State's judicial hierarchy. The highest force in the world is God. He is the Lord of the Princes, who are under him as His vassals. The ruler is not absolutely sovereign, except with regard to his subjects. He himself is bound to God and His commandments just as the subject is to those of the ruler. The right to govern radiates out over the pyramid of State offices, from the ruler down to his subjects. Conversely, the course of obligation moves as follows: "Just as the contracts and testaments [30] of the subjects cannot alter the ordinances of the magistrate, just as the edicts of the magistrate cannot alter those of custom, just as custom cannot alter the laws of the sovereign prince, so too are the laws of the sovereign prince unable to alter the laws of God and of Nature." In Christian belief, this rigid system for the emanation of divine will through the ranks of power is only loosened by God's immediacy for man: The king is subject to God alone, but the magistrates are bound to God and to the king, the subjects to God (for He must always come first), the king, and to the magistrates. At this point, i.e., in the recognition of the human person in his immediacy to

God, the sacro-political hierarchy deviates from the symbolism of Akhenaton in which the ruler is the exclusive intermediary between God and man. As for the rest, Bodin's hierarchy has remained the symbol for internal State order down to the recent secular theories of legal levels. The State's immanent hierarchy of offices and regulations has become self-evident and, after the decapitation of God, could be combined with any sort of legitimizing symbolism whatsoever.

EKKLESIA

In the symbolism of the hierarchy, the State is not a self-contained entity, but rather is dispersed over all the levels of government. These levels extend beyond the earthly ruler to God. The person of the subject is certainly in danger here of being cut off from God by the intermediary functions of the hierarchy; but even if the immediacy of the hierarchy is not expressly granted, as in Bodin, there is still a single, divine flow of power that flows out of the source, over the steps of the pyramid, down to its base. The ruling 🔲 order is suffused with sacred blood, but it is not itself the most sacred of all. The deification of the earthly ruling order, i.e., its world-immanent formulation and the simultaneous decapitation of the world-transcendent God, is bound up with a large number of preconditions.

The formulation of a feudally organized community demands above all, that the community be experienced as an entity with a center of existence resting within itself. In the primitive period, the natural starting point for the growth of a particular, world-immanent, sacro-political community is always the matriarchal or patriarchal ancestral community. Its symbolic world presents itself in countless vestiges in the histories of advanced cultures right down to our own age. The Greek *polis* was still firmly founded upon the idea of an alliance of family cult-units and so the entrance into the State alliance could take place only by way of acceptance into the family cult-unit. In addition—and probably under oriental influence—there was in the Greek as well as in the Egyptian world the personal, apolitical religiosity of the mysteries. The politico-religious tragedy of Socrates, the man who was called by the divine voice of his *daimon* and by the mandate of the oracle at Delphi to carry out the politico-religious reform of his *polis*, is thus performed in the full light of history. He refused to flee, because for him an existence outside of the sacred community was meaningless. A recent historian has determined in him, as in Plato and Aristotle, a less developed level of spirituality compared to that of the Christian era, because it was as yet impossible for these philosophers to breach the bounds of the sacro-political, world-immanent community and to recognize the possibility of an unmediated religious existence in God.

Modern, world-immanent political units are much more strongly and clearly [32] determined by the transformation of the *Ekklesia*-substance than through the vestigial symbols of the tribal community. The Christian idea, as it is developed in the epistles of St. Paul and in the closely related Epistle to the Hebrews, understands *Ekklesia* to be the community as the mystical body of Christ. By several transmutations, the organic analogy is transformed. At one point, the offices of the *Ekklesia* are related as the limbs of a body and complement one another to form the unity of the earthly body whose *Pneuma* is Christ. At another point, the body analogy is carried beyond the visible earthly limbs of the body to Christ Himself, who becomes the head of the body; conversely, the spiritual content can predominate again, in which case the *Pneuma* of Christ flows by the power of His *Pleroma*, that is, His fullness, into the earthly members, so that the personhood of the Savior's *Pneuma* is almost annulled. The analogy is supported by such vestigial ancestral symbolism as the idea of Christ as the second Adam, the second father of man, and by the form of the Supper, which is closely related to the mystery cults. The Pauline variations demonstrate the possibilities for further development.

The *charismata*, which flow out of the *Pneuma* of Christ and which bestow on the members of the body their function, can be extended beyond the scheme for ranks in the original community sketched by Paul to complement political and administrative functions. The office of the ruler acquires its status in the *Corpus Mysticum* and is thus no longer differentiated from the functions of priests and teachers. No boundary separates the political and the religious spheres. The *Corpus Mysticum* constitutes an internally differentiated entity in which there is a sacrament for annointing the king alongside the sacrament for ordaining priests. The performance of the king's office is a sacred function alongside others. Historically this possibility materialized to some extent in the *sacrum imperium* of the ninth century. [33]

Other forms combine with the possibility of developing a hierarchy among the offices of the *Corpus Mysticum*. Accordingly, one of the offices becomes the highest, and the others only have their place in the *corpus* through its mediation and its *charismata*, as in the idea of papal supremacy over the ruler. On the other hand, the immediacy of God's functions can once again be elevated to a principle as in Dante's idea of the emperor. Further, the symbol of a community constituted through the *Pneuma* of Christ can be essentially transformed into intramundane bodies whenever the spiritual entity that has become reality is invested with natural content. This possibility is already evident in the early Christian centuries, when the *Ekklesia* of Christ, as the *populus Christianus*, becomes a nation among nations. The historic sources for this later transformation were the classical empire of divine humans and the bonding of the ruler to the people through the *acclamatio* of the *populus Romanus* and through the Teutonic ideas of tribe and king.

The *Ekklesia* constituted by Christ has changed in myriad ways. Through all transformations, however, the basic structure, which is what concerns us, remains recognizable. The Christian churches have developed directly from it. Yet, to judge by certain of its parts, the idea has remained alive even in the State communities. We participate in the continuity of the *Ekklesia* whenever particular communities that have become world-immanent recognize the equality and brotherhood of all members of the community. This is true even where communities and movements take a sharply anti-clerical and anti-Christian position, and introduce, for example, a new State religion, as in the French Revolution. The continued existence of the Christian community of love in French *solidarite* was recognized by secular philosophers of the Third Republic, and the idea of solidarity [34] was interpreted as a secularized Christian *Caritas*. The Pauline idea of the articulation of the *Corpus Mysticum* as the mutually complementary functions of the community, influenced the theories on the division of labor of the English and French economists and sociologists. The strong, ecclesiastic success of the American national community is well known. As a consequence of the Puritan tradition, the ideas have not changed as much, and we find a Pauline category such as likemindedness, the likemindedness of the members of the body, developed in science as a basic sociological concept. Here too, as a result of the special socio-historical position of the United States, the idea of equality has been more sharply transformed into the idea that only the truly equal in spirit can be full members of the community. The secular *Ekklesia*, which constitutes the community of equals, reacts with particular sensitivity to any threat to its spirit. Educational psychology and the striving for assimilation are the means created to unite the heterogeneous elements that built up the natural *corpus* in the age of immigration into a spiritual *corpus*. Even where the secular *Ekklesia* finds itself in a sharp debate with the Christian Church on religious matters, as in German National Socialism, even there, the basic form of mystical *corpus*, bound by the *Pneuma* into an entity, lives in the furtherance of spiritual conformity, just as Christ in *Caritas* lives in the secularized forms of charitable works for the poor.

SPIRITUAL AND TEMPORAL

One of the most important factors in the formation of the intramundane communities was the split in the *Ekklesia* along [35] spiritual and temporal lines. The opposition expressed itself historically, through more than one dyad, and so we can touch on but two or three main types.

The first great historical-philosophical interpretation of the problem was given by Augustine. World history is the powerful debate between the heavenly and the

earthly *Civitas*, between the Kingdom of Christ and the
Kingdom of Evil. The two realms are not to be
understood as institutions, as perhaps Church and
State (even if one finds occasionally in Augustine the
tendency to understand the State as the *magnum
latrocinium*), but rather as communities of Christ's
followers and of His enemies. The *civitas terrena* is
separated from the *civitas Dei* by the fall of the wicked
angels. The *civitas Dei* begins as an angelic state and
ends as the Kingdom of God; its citizens are all living
creatures created in God's image. The Church is the
representative of God's State on Earth; but even citizens
of the *civitas terrena* are among its sacramentally
bound members, and outside of the Church there are
citizens of the *civitas Dei*. The development of the
symbols took place in an age of conflict for Christendom,
occasioned by the conquest of Rome by the Visigoths
(410). It is directed against an idea that was endangering
the Church, namely that Christendom, i.e., the young
State religion of the Roman Empire, failed to protect
the State against the misfortune. In order to counter
this dangerous public opinion, that Christendom is a
life and accident insurance, Augustine developed the
symbol of true Christian behavior and the meaning of
Christ's following.

As a system, this great conception is very complex
and not fully worked out everywhere; the future
problem can be glimpsed. The *civitas Dei* is neither
identical with the Church nor with the era which

dawned with the redemptive act of Christ; nor is it identical with the eternal Sabbath of the divine final Kingdom. It embraces, entirely or in part, all of these and in addition, [36] the pre-Christian followers of God. It is filled to the extreme with tensions which result from the fact that the institutional elements of the Church are forced together with the apocalyptic elements of the new age of the world and with the eschatological elements of the final Kingdom. The result is a multitude of dualisms: sacramental communities of the Church and its surroundings, mundane-this-worldly and spiritual-other-worldly membership in the *civitas Dei*, the Kingdom of God and the Kingdom of the Devil. Finally, the institutional reality of the State has an ambiguous place in the system, as does the idea that for the good of the world, kingdoms would best be numerous and small, coalescing like the way numerous families of citizens do to form a city.

The tension in the system reflects the tension in the conflict in which Christendom finds itself. There are still no basic schemes for the opposition of spiritual and worldly power in the institutions of Church and State, and of this-worldly and other-worldly personal life. Instead, there are hard, life-despising phrases, as when Augustine responds to the laments over the Roman massacre: "Many perished in all sorts of gruesome ways. Even if one must bemoan this, it is still the common lot of all who are born into this life. As far

as I know, no one died who would not have had to die
sometime anyway.'' Today, words of this sort are found
once again in politico-religious communities, as when
Ernst Junger speaks against the horrible destruction of
life during the war, saying death is bitter whenever it
strikes. Death is a hardship which becomes legitimate
in faith: "Those who fell, went, in falling, from an
incomplete to a complete reality, from Germany of a
temporal nature into eternal Germany."

The problem reveals itself more strictly and more
sharply at the height of scholasticism, when fissures in
the *sacrum imperium* are already visible in the political
theory of Thomas Aquinas. [37] The offices within the
great *Ekklesia* have taken hold and become mutually
independent. The dissolution of the kingdom through
the formation of a great feudal organization has begun:
the feudal Church originates as the first "State in the
Realm"; following it in the institutional transformation
are the princes, the foremost and most radical of whom
was Frederick II of Sicily. The reception of Aristotelian
political theory allows Thomas to determine the
relationship between the functions of the Church and
the princes. Following the *Politics*, Thomas attributes
to the prince the task of exercising secular rule over his
subjects, so that their material and spiritual existence
enables them to pursue their salvation to an optimal
degree; spiritual care is the business of the Church. In
keeping with the higher quality of the spiritual goal as
compared with the temporal, the princely function is

subordinated to the Church in order of degree. The range and the limits of the idea become visible in comparison with Aristotle himself. The Greek philosopher still moves in the politico-religious system of the *polis*. The meaning of personal and national life is understood analogously and the analogy of man and State is expanded to world and God. The most valuable life is the active life of the spirit, for as a spiritually active person, man is most self-sufficient, resembles most the one who is calm within and self-satisfied, and is therefore himself God. Likewise, the autarkic State is best with a life of its own, not too entangled in relations with others, because its self-sustaining life is the analog of divine-cosmic Being. This final state of a spiritualized *polis* religion is in itself complete. Its translation to the Thomistic system allows broad topical areas of Aristotelian politics to endure, but it destroys their central meaning. The cosmos of the divinely analogous State is broken up. The personal and communal existence is divided into two realms and the 38 politico-temporal sphere is overshadowed by the spiritual. The problem of the State institution which was brushed aside by Augustine as unimportant now comes to the fore. It is clearly more a question of the historical situation, when the State institution separates from its subordination to the feudal Church and assumes for itself a sacred meaning. Frederick II had already taken this step. Following the conquest of Jerusalem and his self-elevation to Messiah-King, the emperor speaks as an autocrat, as a heathen God-man. Classical *justitia* is declared to be a State virtue, its cult a State religion. The people are forced to serve and the triumphal arch of Capua is erected as an altar. The Pope declares the emperor to be the Anti-Christ. The first secular political religion had sprouted on the soil of the Christian *Ekklesia*.

THE APOCALYPSE

We have just touched upon particular characteristic phases in the differentation of the *Ekklesia* and in its history in order to show how the politico-religious, symbolic world was built up and how it remains visible as the basic structure of European development up to the present. History was, therefore, viewed from without, as a consequence of changes in a religious symbolic world. We now turn to a new symbolic dimension, to the interpretations of the development from within, i.e., from the point of view of the participating men and powers.

The basic scheme for the religious interpretation of history is already contained in the Pauline division of world history into three spheres: that of the heathen *lex naturalis*, the *lex mosaica* of the Old Testament, and the third, that of the Christian Kingdom. From this beginning, the interpretation develops [39] further by taking up the historical themes deemed important for each age. The development reaches its apex in the German symbolism of the 12th century, in the proclamation of the third realm in that century by Joachim of Flora, and from there to Dante. The interpretation of history is symbolic insofar as the themes are arranged and interpreted as the expression of divine will in history. The rational scheme of ordering is the holy numbers: the number three of the Trinity, the number seven for the gifts of the Holy Spirit, the Hexameron, the six days of Creation, the Old Testament number of forty-two generations from Abraham to Christ, and half this number, the twenty-one generations before Abraham.

The first great Christian historical philosophy to work with the tools of symbolism, the Augustinian, has already been touched upon: the age of Christ is the sixth and at the same time the last earthly one. The holy, final Kingdom of the Beyond follows as the seventh. In the blossoming of German symbolism in the 12th century, the method is completed, only to undergo that change in Joachim of Flora which has become of decisive importance for the dynamics of the *Ekklesia* and for its secular offshoots. Joachim found the formula for a psychic and rational direction which for a long time has sought and found public acceptance. According to this formula, the Kingdom of Christ is not, as in the older division, the last earthly one. Rather it is to be followed by a third one. The first in this numbering system is the divine one of the Old

Covenant; the second, the Christian; the third, that of the third divine person, the Holy Spirit, which coincides with the seventh age of the world, after which there follows the eternal Sabbath of the final Kingdom. Each of these kingdoms is itself divided into seven ages; these ages of the pre-Christian as well as the Christian Kingdom, for which there is historical evidence, are symbolically determined by their leaders. Christ stands at the beginning of the second kingdom, after his predecessors Zacharia and John.

At the beginning of the [40] third kingdom, which stands before us, there is a phenomenon which is called simply DUX, i.e., "Fuhrer." Joachim calculates the advent of the third kingdom to be 1200; the Franciscan clerics of Joachim calculate it to be 1260. The historical models which supported the apocalypse of the third kingdom were the founding of orders, the new religious ones, in which the increasing development of the perfect life in the Holy Spirit became visible. The revelation coalesces during the first generations of Franciscans to the interpretation that St. Francis of Assisi is the prophesied *Dux* and that Joachim and Dominic are his predecessors; the work of Joachim is recognized as the *evangelium aeternum* of the Apocalypse (14, 6). The third kingdom of Joachim is not a new institution which in a revolutionary way would have to take the place of the Church, but rather a process of spiritualization of the *Ekklesia* and the transformation of the World Church into a new order of contemplative, spiritualized monasticism. In contrast to the "Kingdom of the Apocalypse" of Paul, the revelation of Joachim therefore contains no indications as to the social ordering of the third kingdom. In the kingdom of *spiritualis intellegentia* live contemplative men; no longer actively contemplative as in the clergy of the World Church, they live spiritually and in poverty, as brothers, all of the same rank, without a compulsory hierarchy.

The Christian "Kingdom of the Apocalypse" and the symbolism of the late Middle Ages form the deep historical foundation for the apocalyptic dynamism in modern political religions. The movement of the Christian orders since Benedict—above all the movement of the Order of Mendicant Friars—and the founding of new sects within Christendom, has produced the psychic mien for the renewal of the spirit and for collaboration on the perfection of the Christian ideal of existence as a this-worldly one. The increasing rank of perfection of spiritual Being has become one of the strongest elements of secular dynamism since the Renaissance. [41] Examples are the belief in the perfectibility of the human intellect and in the unending upward development of mankind to the ideal final State of the Enlightenment, the deistic founding of Masonic orders for the perfection of the world, and the belief in progress as the religion of the masses in the 19th century. The symbolism of the "Kingdom of the Apocalypse" lives on in the symbolism of the 19th and

20th centuries, in the three kingdoms of Marx-Engelian historical philosophy, in the Third Reich of National Socialism, and in the fascist third Rome that follows the Classical and Christian. Even the thematic determinants of the Third Reich have remained: examples are faith in the dissolution of the world-Church institution through spiritualization into orders of perfect life in the Holy Spirit; belief in the mortality of the State and the free brotherly association of man in the communist third realm; faith in the deliverer of the Kingdom, Dante's five hundred, five and ten (DVX), in the *Führer* figures and myths of our age; and the sects of the new Kingdom in the communist, fascist, and national-socialist *Bunde* and elites as the kernel of the new *Reich's* organizations.

IV

THE LEVIATHAN

The process whereby the western *Ekklesia* dissolves into national, partial communities passes through the Middle Ages and makes itself clearly felt in the Age of Absolutism with the organizational demarcation of the states vis-à-vis one another. Not all regions of Europe reach [42] this point at the same time: the western nation-states were the bearers of the development and have remained the major prototypes to this day. In them too, the theology of the new *Ekklesia* was first thought of as a particular community alongside others, temporal-political and sacred in such an intimate combination, State and Church in such a close unity, that the temporal and spiritual opposites were meaningless.

The great theologian of the particular *Ekklesia*, which was immediately next to God, was Hobbes. He is often regarded as the theoretician of absolute monarchy. Indeed he was that too, but he was more; for he created the symbol of the Leviathan, i.e., of the omnipotent State, situated immediately under God, and in the divine service of its subjects.* The creation of the symbol is accomplished in two stages, first in the natural formation of the statesman, which he claims to be binding for all time; and then historically in the formation of a natural unity, as in the Christian *Ekklesia* of the 17th century. In order to build up the new natural entity of the political nation, Hobbes avails himself of a contractual theory from the biblical tradition of the Old Testament. Men are supposed to have mutually obligated themselves in their natural condition through a contract according to which majority rule sets a sovereign above themselves and transfers all power to him. Hobbes has been called a contractual theorist because of this construction. This is not false, but it refers only to a traditional and time-bound instrument of his theory, not its essence. The essential can be [43] deduced from the formulation for the result of the contract: the previously formless multitude of people does not elect a ruler for itself, but rather combines its majority in the entity of one person; the multitude becomes the entity of the "Commonwealth" by creating for itself a bearer of personality; the Commonwealth, not the elected sovereign, not the person who from now on steps forward as the Actor of History.

*Hobbes has taken the symbol of the Leviathan from the Bible. In Job, Chapters 40 and 41 the monster is described: "His heart is as firm as a stone; yea, as hard as a piece of the nether millstone. When he raiseth up himself, the mighty are afraid: by reason of breakings they purify themselves." "Upon earth there is not his like, who is made without fear. He beholdeth all high things: he is a king over all the children of pride."

We have already stated that the most important prerequisite for the genesis of the secular community's religion was the understanding of a community as a self-centered entity. Hobbes' symbol of the Leviathan takes a decisive step in this direction. To be sure, Hobbes does not achieve the rounded, cosmic-analogous compactness of the Aristotelian *polis* symbol, but the open structure of the Christian *Ekklesia* is to a great extent ended. To be sure, the hierarchy still extends to God and the Commonwealth originates in accordance with the will of God. From God the hierarchy no longer descends to persons who occupy the ranks of the *Ekklesia*, but rather to the community as a collective person. It falls upon the sovereign not as the ruler over his subjects, but rather as the personality-bearer of the Commonwealth.

If one wished to draw historical comparisons, then Hobbes' position with regard to the particular, secular *Ekklesia* would be similar to Paul's position with regard to the creation of symbols for the Christian community. The new community achieves its unity through the sovereign in the same symbolic-mystic manner as does the Pauline *Ekklesia* through the *Pneuma* and *Kephale* of Christ. The secular substrata of the Commonwealth are the particular nations, but their unity is a *corpus mysticum* like the Christian. The histories of the Germanic peoples during the time of the migrations offer the only parallels to this process within European development in a narrower sense. Here we encounter, just as in the case of Hobbes, the creation of the person of a tribe through the crowning of a king [44] and the extinction of the person through his death. The link between "rex" and "gens" is so close that investiture or loss of the king is synonymous with the gain or loss of the unmediated existence—from a traditional point of view—of the natural Being. In the same sense, Hobbes' contract of the ruler creates the State as an historical person, as the "mortal God," the earthly God to whom man is indebted alongside the "Immortal God," for his peace and security.

The Commonwealth is formed not only as a cosmos of political power, but also spiritually, because the sovereign, be he a monarch or a parliament, has the right to judge which opinions and teachings are appropriate to preserve and thus further the unity of the Commonwealth. It is his to decide which individuals and to what extent they are permitted to speak at assemblies; and he must exercise prior censorship over printed works. The justification could have been written by a modern propaganda minister: man's actions are determined by his opinions and whoever guides these opinions correctly, directs the actions towards peace and harmony.

Thus far, the Leviathan is a pagan-sacred symbol. To make it a Christian one requires debate with the previous symbol of the Christian *Ekklesia* and differentiation from it. The extremely scholastic formulation of Thomas, in which the temporal order was subordinated to the spiritual and distinguished from it on an organizational basis, now collapses. The secular order is filled with national interests, becoming a self-seeking entity. The polemics of Hobbes therefore directs itself against the vestige of the *sacrum imperium*, against the Catholic Church, which still lays claim to the personal representation of Christianity [45] and to spiritual pre-eminence. He applies his theory of the Commonwealth to demonstrate that the Church is not a commonwealth and does not have a personality; and that therefore the new *Ekklesia* cannot be a part of an all-embracing Kingdom of God, but is rather an individual person next to God. Hobbes fervently refutes the Pauline idea of Kingdom which, augmented by the king's charisma, dominated the 9th century and according to which the Pope, Emperor, King, Cleric, and Laity are all members of an *Ekklesia*: it would lead to the absurd conclusion that indisputable, historical communal-persons such as France, Spain, Venice would be deprived of their character as persons and made members of the *Ekklesia*. Each commonwealth is in itself a Christian *Ekklesia* when its sovereign makes the Bible and Christianity binding through State law. The State, then, is at the same time a Church, with the sovereign as head of the Church, immediately under God, without the intercession of the Vicar of Christ. A spiritual commonwealth that is a Church and not a State is a contradiction; the distinction between spiritual and temporal was only brought into the world to confuse people, to make subjects repulsive to their sovereign, and to disturb the peace of the Commonwealth-Church.

Hobbes defends his symbol by referring to the story of the Old and the New Covenant. With great fury, the religious potency of Jewish theocracy floods the world of the English Reformation to fuse with the national consciousness in the symbol of the sacred communal person. The stages of Jewish history are carefully traced from the Covenant of Abraham and the submission of Israel to God, through the leadership of Moses and his successors, to the crisis of the decline, when Israel renounces God as its Lord in order to have a king like the other nations. On the example of Abraham, the image of the spiritual head of State [46] is developed. God spoke to Abraham alone, without mediation, as the personality-bearer of his people. For this reason, every subject in the commonwealth, as one to whom God has not revealed himself directly, has to submit to the law of the sovereign in all outward religious acts and confessions. Only in feelings and in thoughts which do not appear outwardly and which cannot be known by the human ruler, is the subject free and responsible to God alone.

The sovereign of the Christian commonwealth occupies the same position as Abraham to his family: God speaks only to him; he alone knows His will, and he alone is justified in interpreting the word and the will of God. With the Jewish-theocratic idea as a model, the symbol of the Leviathan assumes features that are related to those of the State religion of Akhenaton. Once again, the ruler becomes a mediator for God; God reveals Himself to him alone; he alone mediates the will of God to the people—with the sole reservation that a vestige of the personality of man, which is immediate to God, is retained in his private, spiritual life.

The appearance of Christ changes nothing as far as this situation is concerned. Its purpose was the renewal of the covenant with God, which had been broken in the rebellion through the election of King Saul. Christ was sent to redeem man from the sin of the rebellion and to lead him back to the Kingdom of God. This Kingdom, however, is a Kingdom of mercy and not of this world. Only after the Resurrection will Christ begin to rule as king. Ecclesiastic power in this world passed from Christ to the Apostles, from these to their successors through a laying on of hands, until sovereigns accepted Christianity by submitting themselves, not to the Apostles, but rather to God, without intercession, as the One revealed. Christian rulers are in possession of ecclesiastic power, and, through their mediation, God's rule [47] over the *Ekklesiae* subordinated to them in this world is restored.

The new *Ekklesia* is in a struggle with the old Christian one and, being divinely ordained, has to succeed against demands that can only be understood as the work of the Devil. Hobbes must therefore counterbalance the symbol of the Leviathan with that of the satanic Kingdom. As far as Christians are concerned, they fall into the *Ekklesiae* of Christian political communities. The attempt to maintain or to create a universal Christian *Ekklesiae* as an institution with personality is understood as the work of Satan. The Catholic Church, with its claim to spiritual supremacy over all Christians, is the Kingdom of Darkness which wants to disrupt the direct continuation of the idea of God's people from the age of the Jews before the time of the King to the time of the Christian commonwealth. The State is the Church, and whoever appears as the enemy of this new *Ekklesia*, i.e., the Leviathan, is Satan—just as in Jewish history, Palestine was the Kingdom of God and the neighboring nations were the Kingdom of the archenemy, the Devil.

This opposition was maintained for a long time in England. Defoe wrote a voluminous political history of the Devil; and even in 1851, Cardinal Newman thought it necessary to set forth the irrationality of a Satanic interpretation of the Catholic Church by sketching— on the basis of statements from Blackstone's Commentary to the English Constitution—a picture of the English State as a Kingdom of the Devil, corresponding to the pictures of the Devil in anti-Catholic literature, in order to show that this process could be applied at will. The Cardinal's satire is surpassed by reality: the Devil symbol of Hobbes has demonstrated its ability to take on any historical content at will, just as the symbol of the Commonwealth can. The politico-religious history of Europe saw the further development of the particular *Ekklesia* into an ⟦48⟧ intramundane, closed one, and brought forth the corresponding Kingdom of the Devil.

V

THE TEMPORAL COMMUNITY

In its essential features, European politico-religious symbolism has not changed appreciably since the 17th century. Hierarchy and orders, the universal and the particular *Ekklesia*, the Kingdom of God and the Kingdom of the Devil, *Fuhrertum* and Apocalypse remain the forms of language in the religion of the community up to the present. By contrast, their meanings have slowly changed in the direction which the Leviathan specified. The *Ekklesia* withdraws more and more from the union with the universal Kingdom, with its hierarchic apex in God, until it becomes autonomous in individual instances and closes as a temporal reality. It is no longer divinely infused by the Supreme Source, but rather has itself become primal, sacred substance. Vestiges of the old division are still retained in unimportant formulae. For example, the sacred, closed community acts according to the mandate of God when it propagates on earth; but the "mandate of God" is synonymous with intramundane formulae such as "the mandate of history," "historical imperative," the "mandate of blood," etc. We therefore have only to supplement previously drawn lines and to point to symptoms of the new investment of content.

These are known facts to everyone, but are rarely interpreted as expressions of political religiosity.

The strong foundation of the new temporality which has been developing in the centuries since the late Middle Ages, is the interpretation of the world as a store of existential facts of all 49 degrees, and as the knowledge of its essential and causal relationships. The knowledge of space and of nature, of the earth and of the peoples who inhabit it, of their history and spiritual differentiation, of plants and animals, of man as corporeal being and as spiritual, of his historical existence and his intellectual ability, of the life of his soul and of his drives, this knowledge permeates to a massive extent the new view of the world and forces all knowledge of divine order to one side and beyond. Schelling's radical metaphysical question: Why is there Something; why is there not Nothing? — is the concern of few; for the large masses it means nothing for their religious attitude. The world as content has displaced the world as existence. The methods of science become the generally applicable forms for the study of the world's content. Man's attitude towards the world must be based on these. Since the 19th century, and in great periods up to the present, the word "metaphysical" has become a curse-word. In a new twist, religion as the "opium of the people" has become an "illusion" with a dubious future. Formulae arise that are contrary to those of spiritual religions and to their view of the world. They justify themselves on the basis of world science as the valid form of insight in contrast to revelation and mystical thought. There arise "scientific philosophies," "scientific socialism," "scientific racial theory." The "world riddles" are catalogued and resolved. At the same time knowledge of the fundamental questions of Being and of the forms of language, in which they are treated, declines as general knowledge and withdraws into a small circle. Indifference, a laissez-faire attitude, and theism become the hallmarks of a publicly applicable world-view.

Men allow the world content to grow to such a proportion that the world and God disappear behind it, but they cannot eliminate the problematics of their own existence. It lives on in [50] each individual soul, and when God has become invisible behind the world, then the things of the world become new gods. When the symbols of transcendental religiosity are banned, new symbols, developed out of the intramundane scientific language, take their place. The temporal community has its apocalypse just as the Christian *Ekklesia*, except that the new prophets of the apocalypse assert that their symbolic creations are scientific judgements. We have already drawn a few lines from the Joachitic symbolism up to modern times, in order to call attention to the continuity of linguistic forms. The secular apocalypse need only remove from the Joachitic system the transcendental final Kingdom, the eternal Sabbath, the Beyond, to have at its disposal the symbolic language appropriate to the inner world. The final Kingdom is no longer a supernatural community of the spirit, but rather an earthly condition of perfected humanity.

Kant's ideas on history, in a cosmopolitan sense, sketch a picture of history in which the rational being, as a temporal person, ascends to higher and higher levels of perfection until finally he progresses under appropriate leaders to the cosmopolitan community which is free from compulsion. Mankind is the great collectivity towards whose development each individual has to contribute his share. It is concluded on earth and only as a whole does it strive forward; the significance of the individual existence is in its instrumental effect on collective progress. The formula is radically collective, so radical in fact that Kant expressed astonishment, vis-à-vis his own formulation, that man does not profit from his activity for the collectivity, but rather only later generations which enter into the perfection of the earthly paradise. Christian objections arise and Kant finds a way out in the idea of personal immortality, even though his reader has the impression that it did not seem to him [51] to be an adequate enough substitute for the earthly life of the complete, rational person.

Kant's revelation is humane—other prophets of the apocalypse confine their symbolism to the mission of a particular community. Fichte develops his revelation in relationship to the symbolism of the Gospel according to John: the final Kingdom, as an earthly one, is the Kingdom of God, and the only people able to regenerate mankind and to introduce the Kingdom of God is the original German *Volk*. Comte expands the theories of Vico and Saint-Simon to the law of the three historical stages of the world—the religious, the metaphysical, and the upcoming positivist-scientific—and finds that the French are the bearers of the positivist spirit. Marx divides history into the pre-communist age, the class-state, and the final communist age and recognizes the proletariat as the bearer of the development towards the final Kingdom. Racial theorists since Gobineau interpret world history as a movement and struggle of the races and see a select Nordic or Germanic race as the bearer.

Each of the apocalypses in European history has created its Devil symbolism too. We have already spoken about the Catholic Church as the Satan corresponding to the Leviathan. Kant's Devil is human instinct. Fichte sketched Napoleon as the monstrous figure of Satan. Religion and metaphysics belong to the positivist apocalypse as Evil; the bourgeoisie to the proletariat; the minority, above all the Jews as the "opposing race," to the select racist apocalypse.

The common feature of the new symbolism is its "scientific" character. A peculiar dynamism results, which in the course of less than a century has greatly changed the spiritual structure of the temporal community. The apocalypses which we have just enumerated are "naive," i.e., they claim in good faith the character of scientific judgements for their theses.

Beginning in the middle 52 of the 19th century and
emanating from Marxism, criticism of the Apocalypse
under the title of the examination of ideologies became
ever more radical. The examiners wanted to prove that
the symbolic systems did not correspond to the demands
of scientific methodology, and that they were formed by
certain positions of interest. With its claim to be
scientific analysis, the Apocalypse takes a stand on the
basis of scientific discussion and is analyzed from the
point of view of its own prerequisites.

Now, one might believe that, as a consequence of the
reciprocal exposure of ideological criticism, the way
would be open for the return to firmer, more critical
views of the world. But something remarkable
happened: the attitude of temporal religiosity is so
strong, that its apocalypses have not crumbled under
the attack of scientific criticism, but rather its concept
of truth has been modified. In the first phase of this
development the unscientific character of the symbols
is recognized. The politico-religious individual,
however, does not permit himself to be defeated on this
account. Rather the symbol is retained in consideration
of its value to unite the masses, even though it is
scientifically inadequate. A conscious apocalypse takes
the place of naive a one. In place of the system which
purports to be rationally theoretical, nationally
economic or sociological, one finds the "myth": the
myth is consciously engendered in order to unite the
masses affectively and to transpose them into politically

effective states, in which they expect redemption. Since the myth is not justified by supernatural revelation and scientific criticism cannot stand its ground, there develops in the second phase a new concept of truth— Rosenberg's concept of so-called organic truth. We already find the beginnings in Hobbes' thesis that a teaching which disturbs the unity and the peace of the Commonwealth cannot be true. The theory is then further developed into the interpretation, that that which promotes the existence of the organically closed [53] temporal community of a people is true. Knowledge and art, myth and mores are true when they are in the service of the populace united by race. "From thence they come and thence they shall return. And in this they all find their decisive criterion, whether they increase the form and inner worth of this race of people, cultivate it to a position of greater esteem, form it in a more vital manner or not." Myth formation is thus withdrawn from the field of rational discussion and approaches actual symbolism as a sphere of sentient forms, in which world-immanent experience and transcendental experience combine to form a comprehensible unity.

The pragmatic aspect of this world-immanent persuasion has as a consequence that the person of this religious type is prepared to know the psychological technique of myth-engendering, its propaganda and social dissemination, but not willing to allow this knowledge to disturb him in his faith. When that which promotes the community is true, then so too are the means that carry out the myth that furthers the community—not only the correct ones in the technical sense, but also the permitted and indeed the prescribed ones in the communal, religious sense. It was therefore possible to develop the technique of myth-propaganda to its present high level, without having the fact of its being propaganda destroy its own purpose. The insights of depth-psychology into the instinctive life of the individual and the masses could be put to good use technically, without this appeal to the instincts evoking resistance. This insight into the motivation for instincts has led just as little to a rationalization of the personality as ideological criticism has to the destruction of the intramundane belief in revelation. On the contrary, it has led to the recognition that hate is stronger than love, and for that reason, the unleashing of the aggressive instincts and the buildup of attitudes of hate are the means at one's disposal for the realization of the community-goals. [54]

This important phenomenon becomes clearer in its effect as the distinguishing characteristic of temporal religiosity when we compare it to a view of supernatural means to an end, as in Ignatius of Loyola. The views of Ignatius deal with the coordination of the correct means to live for a creature to attain its sole goal: the honor of God and the salvation of the soul. To this end, the means which are to serve this purpose must be chosen ''so that I do not subordinate and forcefully subject the end to the means, but rather the means to the end." In clear awareness of human instinct, the careful test is recommended: did any conduct correspond to "unordered inclinations," and was it therefore chosen in the hope that God would nonetheless approach the soul, instead of being subordinated as a means completely for the purpose of the soul's salvation and for the honor of God. Conduct, therefore, assumes the position of an earthly means, which derives its significance from the supernatural goal and may contain nothing which is inconsistent with the sacred purpose.

If the intramundane collective existence takes the place of God, the person becomes a serving member of the sacred world-content; he becomes an instrument, as already—and even—Kant remarked with "astonishment": the problem of his life-style, his physical and spiritual existence is only important in relation to the existence of the all-embracing community as *Realissimum*. In an attitude of temporal religiosity, the individual accepts this position; he regards himself as a tool, as an Hegelian cog in the great whole and willingly subordinates himself to the technical means with which the orginazation of the collectivity incorporates him. Knowledge of the world's content and the technical systems founded as a result are not the temporally subordinated means for the eternal goal of life in the world-transcendent God, but rather the life blood of the world-immanent 55 God himself. They

form the *corpus mysticum* of the collectivity and bind
the members into the unity of the body. They are not
condemned as a crime against the dignity of the person;
they are not even merely endured out of insight into the
mandate of the moment. They are demanded and
desired as methods of religio-ecstatic union of the
individual with his God. The engendering of the myth
and its propagation through the newspaper and radio,
through speeches and communal festivals, gatherings
and parades, the planning for and the dying in war, are
the intramundane forms of the *unio mystica*.

SYMBOLISM

The symbolism of the completely closed temporal
Ekklesia needed only to exceed the symbol of the
Leviathan a little—the decisive step was the decapitation
of God. In the symbolism of Hobbes, the majority of
people came together in the unity of the Commonwealth
according to rules of the divinely ordained law; and the
Christian Commonwealth stood below God as a
collective person with the sovereign as mediator to
God. The relationship with the imperial religion of
Akhenaton and the orientation of the symbol to the
people of Abraham's God has already been indicated. In
the complete secular symbolism, the bond with God is
now severed and in its place steps the community itself
as a source of justification for the communal person.

The language of the symbolism is fairly well developed rationally and is even relatively uniform, because the theorists of the two radically temporal *Ekklesiae*, the Fascist Italian and the National-Socialist German, draw on the common vocabulary of German 56 Romanticism. The sacred substance of both is the spirit of the people or the objective spirit, a *Realissimum* lasting through the ages which becomes historical reality in individual men as members of their *Volk* and in their works. Mussolini speaks of Fascism as a religious idea and of the politics of the regime as religious politics, because Fascism proceeds from the assumption that man is in touch with a *Volonta obiettive*, and achieves personality through this connection in a spiritual realm, in the realm of his people.

By reason of this assumption, the structure of the symbolism arises in the forms which Hobbes worked out. The "People" are the "people at large," a community of language, custom, culture, economic trade. They become the "people of the union" through the historical person, through the political organization. In place of the contract-theory of Hobbes and the election of the sovereign there steps another, temporal-sacred selection principle for the bearers of personality in the community. In the Italian as in the German theory, the person of the comrade of the people certainly stands in relation to the spirit of the people, since only through this relation does the comrade of the people have status among the people, as a spiritual body; but the status is not the same for all. In some people, those in the minority, it lives more weakly, and only in one does it express itself completely—in the *Führer*. "The *Führer* is infused by the idea; it manifests itself through him. But he is also the one who is able to give this idea living form. In him, the spirit of the *Volk* is realized and in him the will of the people is formed. In him, the *Volk*, which encompasses generations, and for that reason can never gather tangibly in its entirety, achieves visible form. He is the representative of the people"—writes a German theorist. The *Führer* is the place at which the spirit of the people breaks into historical reality. [57] The temporal God speaks to the *Führer* just as the supernatural God does to Abraham and the *Fürher* transforms the words of God as commands to the narrower following and to the people. Contact with the symbolism of the Leviathan is so close, that even the same words are used to grasp the mystical personification of the *Ekklesia*: The *Führer* in the German theory is the "representative" in the same sense that the sovereign of Hobbes is the representative, the bearer of personality of the Commonwealth. A certain difference exists on this point between Italian and German symbolism, insofar as the spirit of the Italian people is understood more spiritually, while in the German the spirit is linked to blood and the *Führer* becomes the speaker of the spirit of the *Volk* and the representative of the people by virtue of his racial unity with them.

A further element of the theory is not as carefully developed as the foregoing: the difficult point is the personality status of the subjects. On the one hand, they are members of the *Volk* because the spirit of the *Volk* lives in them; on the other hand, they are politically and organizationally in contact with the spirit of the *Volk* through the mediation of the *Führer*. The imperial religion of Akhenaton solved the problem radically, by giving the pharaoh the function of mediator and having the will of God pass down from him to the people. In the temporal symbolism, the *Führer* and the *Volk* share a common bond in the sacred substance which lives in the one as in the other. God is not outside, but rather lives within men themselves; and it would therefore be possible for the spirit of the *Volk* to express itself in the will of the people too, and for the voice of the people to become the voice of God. The theorists overcame the problem by recognizing on the one hand the historical existence of the people as the expression of the spirit of the *Volk* in custom and mores, language and culture, and—especially in the German theory—by interpreting the organization of the State as a structure under whose 58 protection the citizenry can develop accordingly. On the other hand, they reject the political determination of will by the people—once again particularly evident in the German theory: the *Führer* is the only bearer of the will of the people. In the teachings on suffrage of the people, the idea that the act of suffrage is an act of the will of the

people is decisively rejected. Suffrage should outwardly
show and strengthen the agreement between the will of
the people, as objectively embodied in the *Führer*, and
the subjective conviction of those belonging to the
people. Suffrage of the people is an acknowledgement
of the *Führer* and not a proclamation of one's own will.
If, therefore, the vote fails to confirm the will of the
Führer, then the *Führer* need not yield to the will of the
people, since the rejection is not the objective will of
the people, but rather the expression of a subjective
arbitrariness. According to this construct, the symbolism
very strongly approaches that of the Egyptians; God
speaks only to the *Führer*; the people learn of His will
only through the mediation of the *Führer*.

FAITH

The world of symbols is a complete one, an ultimate
one: we want to descend to the sources, to the forces,
which create the symbolic forms. Gerhard Schumann's
"Lieder vom Reich" are one of the strongest expressions
of politico-religious fervor. They make it possible to
follow the movements of the soul, out of whose
substance symbols are constructed, and the historical
reality of the temporal community. As religious
stimulations, they have their roots in the experience of
creatureliness; but the *Realissimum* in which they are
redeemed is not, as in the Christian experience, God,

but rather the people and the brotherhood of the sworn companions. Moreover, the ecstasies are not spiritual, but [59] rather instinctive, and find an outlet in the racial intoxication of the deed. We present the formulae, in which the poet himself expresses his experience.

The basic agitation of creaturely abandonment is described as a condition of dream-like irreality, of coldness, of self-contained loneliness; burning, the soul breaks out of it in order to unite with the divine whole; a hot stream of excitement carries it along, out of its isolation into the brotherhood of "Earth, Light, and Thing." The transition from the attitude of austere pride to this melting and streaming is simultaneously active and passive. The soul wants to and does experience itself as actively penetrating obstacles and it is at the same time driven, carried along by a stream to which it must only give itself over.

The soul has combined with the stream of brotherly worldflow: "And I was One. And the Whole flowed." The stream flows onward, bursting through all walls, and allows the soul to flow into the whole of the people; in finding and in the union, the soul is depersonalized; it frees itself completely from the cold ring of the self; it spreads out beyond its freezing small nature, becomes "good and great"; in the loss of its Self, it ascends into the larger reality of the *Volk*: "Lost myself and found the *Volk*, the *Reich*." In a further vision, the German earth is rejuvenated, a new heaven arches up over it, and out of the chaos rises the Grail, the image of a new

order, in whose service the soul pledges itself with its
companions in a sworn brotherhood. Reality, however,
is still oppressive; time weighs heavily upon the *Reich*;
and those who are austere turn away, magically bound
by their oath, "awaiting the hour of fire which they
deemed fitting." Necessity afflicts even more
oppressively; life hesitates until out of the glow of the
last moment before the collapse the cry of thousands is
heard: "The *Führer!* Slaves that we are, make us
free!" [60]

In a vision reminiscent of that on the Mount of
Olives,—"Then the night came. The One stood and
struggled"—the longed for *Führer* takes up the
command of God, to redeem his people:

> "...And descending
> he bore the torch into the night

> Millions bowed down before him in silence
> Redeemed. The heavens flamed pale as morning.
> The sun grew. And with it grew the *Reich*."

Even this last vision does not overstep the bounds of
religious fervor in the individual soul. The need of the
people and their redemption by the *Führer* are not
historical occurrences in the outside world, which the
orator forms into an image as a poet does. The need is
the need of the soul, which has lost itself ecstatically in
the people; their suffering is its suffering; and the
Führer, who descends from the mountain as the savior
after his struggle with God, in order to redeem the

people, redeems the individual soul, which has sworn itself in service to the Grail, to the building of the cathedral of the *Reich*.

The religious fervor is not assuaged in the union with the whole; it requires the tension of battle and the ecstasy of the deed. The redemptive act of the *Führer* and the victory of the union of sworn ascetics in the empirical founding of the *Reich* present a model according to which what could previously be heard is now unmistakably expressed: namely, that the personal religious drama and the drama of the whole people can be separated. In a time of tension and expectation, the servants of the Grail are the standard-bearers and champions of the coming *Reich*. Once the *Reich* is politically organized, the fervor of the ascetics dissipates in every day tasks and routine concerns, relieved of the struggle. In the poem: "And after the victories come those who celebrate. Then they are great and the soldier is silent." [61] The poet turns against these busy ones, who are superficial and unaware, who want to explain the sense of what has happened, while the warriors, trembling for destiny, inquire about new orders. Furthermore, they are those driven to new battles: "There is no time to pass away in festivals — we are about to forge the new *Reich*." While the others fail to grasp "the destiny, which arises, to be fulfilled." A prayer arises:

"Do not permit me to set up house.

Do not grant me to grow full and exhort rest.

Push me into each despair and unrest of the
heart."

Another verse admonishes: "Push yourself beyond
your desire! Beyond the stars! Upward!" The will to
lose oneself and to break out ecstatically is motivated by
a deep-seated existential *Angst,* as in the "Munster"
poem:

"And all *Angst,* the dreadful fear
Bursts open: from tower to tower, upwards,
upwards!"

The poem, "The Deed," presents the stages of fervor for
the deed, up to its release. The meaningfulness of the
deed is not the victory, but rather the act itself. The
pain, inflicted upon the enemy should rebound into the
soul of the door: "And when you strike, smite your own
heart." Friend and foe alike must be destroyed, to
complete isolation; in the deed, the evil, destructive
deed, the doer smites himself until the extinction of his
own wish and will; the naked, aimless act, the self-
inflicted wound, and laceration are acts of mystical
self-extinction and communion with the world until
the release in the intoxication of blood: "The deed was
good, if you reddened it with blood."

For these doers, those who are marked, the new world
of [62] victory is dull and spiritless. They are homeless
in the everyday world, and at celebrations they feel
alienated:

"In hard glances and in unaffected ones
They carry only scaffolds, no mercy."

Maimed, spiritless, sometimes lifting themselves up, they wait "on the lookout for orders." They find themselves once again out of the mainstream as "a pack of men resolved," bound to one another "because the heart's blood draws the hearts of men to it." They are the core, the soul of the *Reich*, devoted only to the *Führer*, who is lonely, the *Führer*, of whom they dream at night.

> "From their steps echoes the judgement of blood.
> In their soul they carry the Grail.
> Servants of the *Führer*, guardians and avengers alike.
> In them burns, with them grows the *Reich*."

VI

EPILOGUE

We have concerned ourselves, as seekers of truth, with
political religions. For that reason let us draw our first
conclusion about what we have learned: the life of men
in a political community cannot be defined as a profane
sphere, in which we only have to deal with questions of
organizations, of law, and of power. The community is
also a realm of religious order, and the recognition of a
political situation is incomplete in one decisive point if
it does not also embrace the religious forces of the
community and the symbols in [63] which they find
expression; or indeed, if it embraces them but does not
recognize them as such, but rather translates them into
a-religious categories. Man lives in the political
community with all aspects of his being from the
corporeal to the spiritual and religious. To make this
clear, we have drawn examples only from the
Mediterranean and Western European cultural sphere,
but this thesis is meant to be a general one and is just as
valid for the political forms of the East. The political
community is always arranged in relatioship to man's
experience of world and God, be it that the political
sphere assumes in the hierarchy of Being a lower degree
of divine order, be it that it is itself deified. The
language of politics, too, is always infused with the

fervor of religiosity, becoming hereby the symbol, in a precise sense, of the penetration of secular experience by the transcendental-divine. In each of the high cultures, elements of the symbolism, of the linguistic patterns, can be found, which we have developed on the basis of Mediterranean-European examples: the hierarchy, in which the sacred substance speaks out from the supernatural God to the community of creatures; the *Ekklesia* as sacred, communal substance; the Apocalypse as the revelation of the Kingdom; the divine kings as the mediators of God and bearers of personality in the community.

If we now enter the religious sphere itself, then the Christian decision is clear. The Mystic of Frankfurt says in the *German Theology*: "If a creature attributes something good to himself, such as essential nature, life, knowledge, recognition, ability, in short all that, which one would have to call good, as if it were this thing or had it, as if it belonged to it or emanated from it, then it goes astray. What else did the Devil do? What else was the Fall and renunciation for him than that he presumed he too was Something, and claimed to be Someone and his Own. This presumption and his "I" and "Me," his "to Me" and "My"— 64 that was his renunciation and his Fall. And so it continues to be." It is not all the same, how the sphere of human-political organization is arranged in the order of Being. Temporal religiosity, that of the collectivity, be it mankind, the *Volk*, the class, the race, or the State,

which is expressed as the *Realissimum*, is a falling
away from God. And for that reason, many a Christian
philosopher refuses to place the intramundane political
religion on the same level as the spiritual religion of
Christendom, even in speaking. They speak of
demonologies in contrast to the belief in God or of a
faith, which is the work of man, a "mystique humaine,"
as opposed to true faith. The belief in man as the source
of good and of the betterment of the world, such as that
which dominated the Enlightenment, and the belief in
the collective as a mysterious, divine entity, as has been
propagated since the 19th century, is anti-Christian, to
use the language of the Mystic of Frankfurt; it is a
turning away. And in the sense of the undogmatic *vita
contemplativa*, i.e., the view of Being in the stratified
realm from nature to God, the intramundane religiosity
and its symbolism conceals the most essential elements
of reality; it blocks the way to the reality of God and
distorts the relationship between the levels of Being
below God.

Neither this recognition, however, nor the Christian
decision resolves the mystery of God and of His Being.
The divine Creation contains Evil; the majesty of Being
is clouded by the misery of creatures; the order of the
community is built on Hate and Blood, with lament
and in the apostasy from God. Schelling's basic
question about the world: Why is there Something, why
is there not Nothing? is followed by another: "Why is it,
as it is?"—the question of theodicy. [65]

SOURCE NOTES

The historical-factual content of the present essay is based almost exclusively on the sources themselves.

The theoretical assumptions and historical interpretations are not novel, but rather present once again the present position of scholarship. For the reader who wishes to concern himself further with the understanding of individual questions, a few of the main works are indicated which relate to the problems introduced.

The religious-scientific assumptions in general follow Erich Przywara, S.J., *Religionphilosophie katholischer Theologie (Handbuch der Philosophie. Edited by A. Baumler and M. Schroter. Abteilung II. Natur-Geist-Gott)*. Munich and Berlin: Verlag R. Oldenbourg, 1927.

A source for the phenomena of the new mass-religiosity at the close of the 19th century is the work of William James, *The Varieties of Religious Experience: A Study in Human Nature*. London: Longmans, Green & Co., 1902.

For the recognition of present politico-religious phenomena the study of Etienne de Greef, "Le drame humain et la psychologie des 'mystiques' humaines" (contained in *Foi et "Mystiques" Humaines*. Etudes

Carmélitaines. 22 Année. Vol. I. Avril 1937), is important.

The essential philosophical-anthropological views of this author are based on the broad contemporary literature on this subject, easily accessible in the work of Max Scheler, *Die Stellung des Menschen im Kosmos*. Darmstadt: Otto Reichl Verlag, 1928.

The chapter on Akhenaton is based on J.H. Breasted, *Geschichte Ägyptens*. 2nd. edition. Vienna: Phaidon-Verlag, 1936.

For the questions on the European Middle Ages, in particular the problem of Joachim of Flora, see Alois Dempf, *Sacrum Imperium, Geschichts- und Staatsphilosophie des Mittelalters und der politischen Renaissance*. Munich and Berlin: R. Oldenbourg, 1929.

On the problems of the 12th and 13th centuries see further the work of Georges de Lagarde, *LaNaissance de l'esprit laique au déclin du Moyen-Age*. I. and II. Editions Béatrice. 1934. [66]

Further, Ernst Kantorowicza, *Kaiser Friedrich der Zweite*. Berlin: Georg Bondi, 1928.

As far as more recent major attempts to understand the political problem as a religious one are concerned, the author has become aware of only one: Alexander Ular, *Politik. Untersuchungen über die völkerpsychologischen Bedingungen gesellschaftlicher Organisation*. Frankfurt a. M: Rutten and Loenig,

1906. (*Die Gesellschaft. Sammlung sozialpsychologischer Monographien*. Edited by Martin Buber. Volume 3.) [67]

SCHRIFTENREIHE
»AUSBLICKE«

ERICH VOEGELIN

DIE POLITISCHEN RELIGIONEN

1939

BERMANN-FISCHER VERLAG, STOCKHOLM

ERICH VOEGELIN

DIE POLITISCHEN RELIGIONEN

1939

BERMANN-FISCHER VERLAG, STOCKHOLM

VORWORT

Die Abhandlung über die „Politischen Religionen" ist zum ersten
Mal im April 1938 in Wien ausgegeben worden. Die nationalsozia-
listische kommissarische Leitung des Verlages tat nicht viel für die
Verbreitung, so daß die Abhandlung fast unbekannt geblieben ist.
Aber sie wurde bekannt genug, um auch bei verständnisvollen Le-
sern ähnlich kritische Antwort zu finden wie meine früheren Schrif-
ten; man macht mir den Vorwurf, ich sei in der Darstellung so
objektiv, daß sie geradezu für jene Weltbilder und Bewegungen, im
besonderen für den Nationalsozialismus, werbe, die zu bekämpfen
sie bestimmt sei; es fehle die Entschiedenheit des Urteils und der
Verurteilung, die meine eigene Haltung außer Zweifel stellen würde.
Diese Kritiker rühren an Grundfragen der gegenwärtigen Welt-
lage und der Haltung des Einzelnen zu ihr. Es gibt heute einen
Typus des politisierenden Intellektuellen — und jene Kritiker gehören ihm meistens an — der seine tiefe Abneigung gegen den
Nationalsozialismus in kräftigen ethischen Urteilen kundgibt; er
hält es für seine Aufgabe und Pflicht, den Kampf mit allen ihm zur
Verfügung stehenden literarischen Mitteln zu führen. — Das kann
ich auch: meine Abneigung gegen jede Art von politischem Kollektivismus ist für jeden, der lesen kann, aus dem Dantevers zu erkennen, der der Abhandlung vorangeht; und mein Vorrat an gebildeten
und weniger gebildeten Ausdrücken der Verurteilung kann sich
sehen lassen. Daß ich ihn nicht im Rahmen von politisierenden
Ergüssen gegen den Nationalsozialismus vor einer größeren Öffent-

lichkeit ausbreite, hat seine Gründe. Es hat viele Gründe. Ich kann hier nur einen, sehr wesentlichen, berühren.

Der politische Kollektivismus ist nicht nur eine politische und moralische Erscheinung; viel bedeutsamer scheint mir das religiöse Element in ihm zu sein. Der literarische Kampf als ethische Gegenpropaganda ist wichtig, aber er wird bedenklich, wenn er das Wesentliche verdeckt. Doppelt bedenklich: denn er lenkt die Aufmerksamkeit davon ab, daß sich hinter den ethisch verwerflichen Handlungen ein tieferes und gefährlicheres Übel verbirgt; und er wird in seinen eigenen Mitteln wirkungslos und fragwürdig, wenn er keinen tieferen Grund findet als einen sittlichen Kodex. Ich will also nicht sagen, daß der Kampf gegen den Nationalsozialismus nicht auch als ethischer geführt werden soll; er wird nur — nach meiner Ansicht — nicht radikal geführt, weil die radix, die Wurzel in der Religiosität fehlt.

Eine religiöse Betrachtung des Nationalsozialismus muß von der Annahme ausgehen dürfen, daß es Böses in der Welt gebe; und zwar das Böse nicht nur als einen defizienten Modus des Seins, als ein Negatives, sondern als eine echte, in der Welt wirksame Substanz und Kraft. Einer nicht nur sittlich schlechten sondern religiös bösen, satanischen Substanz kann nur aus einer gleich starken religiös guten Kraft der Widerstand geleistet werden. Man kann nicht eine satanische Kraft mit Sittlichkeit und Humanität allein bekämpfen.

Dieser Schwierigkeit aber ist nicht durch einen einfachen Entschluß abzuhelfen. Es gibt heute keinen bedeutenden Denker der westlichen Welt, der nicht wüßte — und es auch ausgesprochen hätte — daß sich diese Welt in einer schweren Krise befindet, in einem Prozeß des Verdorrens, der seine Ursache in der Säkularisierung des Geistes, in der Trennung eines dadurch nur weltlichen Geistes von seinen Wurzeln in der Religiosität hat, und der nicht wüßte, daß die Gesundung nur durch religiöse Erneuerung, sei es im Rahmen der geschichtlichen Kirchen, sei es außerhalb dieses Rahmens, herbeigeführt werden kann. Die Erneuerung kann in großem Maße nur von großen religiösen Persönlichkeiten ausgehen — aber jedem ist es möglich, bereit zu sein und das Seine zu tun, um den Boden zu bereiten, aus dem sich der Widerstand gegen das Böse erhebt.

8

In diesem Punkte nun versagen die politisierenden Intellektuellen völlig. Es ist grauenhaft, immer wieder zu hören, daß der Nationalsozialismus ein Rückfall in die Barbarei, in das dunkle Mittelalter, in Zeiten vor dem neueren Fortschritt zur Humanität sei, ohne daß die Sprecher ahnen, daß die Säkularisierung des Lebens, welche die Humanitätsidee mit sich führte, eben der Boden ist, auf dem antichristliche religiöse Bewegungen wie der Nationalsozialismus erst aufwachsen konnten. Die religiöse Frage ist für diese säkularisierten Geister tabu; und sie ernsthaft und radikal aufzuwerfen scheint ihnen bedenklich — vielleicht auch als eine Barbarei und ein Rückfall in das dunkle Mittelalter.

Wichtiger als mich an jenem ethischen Abwehrkampf zu beteiligen, scheint es mir daher, die religiöse Grundfrage unserer Zeit zu erörtern und das Phänomen des Bösen, das bekämpft werden soll, zu beschreiben. Wenn meine Darstellung den Eindruck erweckt, als sei sie zu „objektiv" und „werbe" für den Nationalsozialismus, so scheint mir dies ein Zeichen dafür zu sein, daß sie gut ist — denn das Luziferische ist nicht schlechthin ein sittlich Negatives, ein Gräuel, sondern eine Kraft, und zwar eine sehr anziehende Kraft; und die Darstellung wäre schlecht, wenn sie den Eindruck hervorriefe, als handle es sich nur um eine sittlich minderwertige, dumme, barbarische, verächtliche Angelegenheit. Daß ich die Kraft des Bösen nicht für eine Kraft des Guten halte, geht für jeden, der für religiöse Fragen nicht stumpf ist, deutlich aus dieser Abhandlung hervor.

Cambridge, Mass. Weihnachten 1938

I.

DAS PROBLEM

Von politischen Religionen zu sprechen und die Bewegungen unserer Zeit nicht nur als politische, sondern auch, und vor allem, als religiöse zu deuten, versteht sich heute noch nicht von selbst, obwohl die Tatbestände den aufmerksamen Beobachter zu dieser Rede zwingen. Der Grund des Widerstandes liegt in dem symbolischen Sprachgebrauch, wie er sich in den letzten Jahrhunderten mit der Auflösung der abendländischen Reichseinheit und dem Werden der modernen Staatenwelt gefestigt hat. Wer von Religion spricht, denkt an die Institution der Kirche, und wer von Politik spricht, denkt an den Staat. Die Organisationen stehen einander als klare, feste Einheiten gegenüber, und der Geist, der diese Körper erfüllt, ist nicht von gleicher Art. Der Staat und der weltliche Geist haben ihren Geltungsbereich im erbitterten Kampf gegen das heilige Reich des Mittelalters erobert, und in der Kampfposition haben sich sprachliche Symbole gebildet, welche nicht die Wirklichkeit als solche erkennen, sondern die Gegensätze des Kampfes festhalten und verteidigen wollen.

Die Begriffe des Religiösen und des Politischen sind den Institutionen und ihren Symbolen gefolgt; sie haben sich auf das Kampffeld begeben und sich unter die Autorität der kämpferischen Sprachsymbole gestellt, so daß heute auch für die Erkenntnis unter dem Drucke ihrer begrifflichen Mittel Gegensätze bestehen, wo vielleicht bei kritischer Prüfung nur unterschiedliche Fälle der Wirksamkeit von nahe verwandten menschlichen Grundkräften zu finden sein werden. Die Begriffe von Religion und Staat, wie sie heute im allgemeinen europäischen Sprachgebrauch, aber auch bis tief in den engeren der Wissenschaft, verbindlich sind, orientieren sich an bestimmten Modellen, die ihre besondere Bedeutung im Geisteskampf Europas haben. Unter Religion versteht man Erscheinungen wie das Christentum und die anderen großen Erlösungsreligionen; unter Staat versteht man die politischen Organisationen vom Typus des modernen Nationalstaates. Um die politischen Religionen angemessen zu erfassen, müssen wir daher den Begriff des Religiösen so erweitern, daß nicht nur die Erlösungsreligionen, sondern auch jene anderen Erscheinungen darunter fallen, die wir in der Staatsentwicklung als religiöse zu erkennen glauben; und wir müssen den Begriff des Staates daraufhin prüfen, ob er wirklich nichts anderes betrifft als weltlich-menschliche Organisationsverhältnisse ohne Beziehung zum Bereich des Religiösen.

STAAT

Eine Schuldefinition, die bisher niemand religiöser Ansprüche verdächtigt hat, sagt vom Staat, er sei eine Verbandseinheit seßhafter Menschen, ausgestattet mit ursprünglicher Herrschermacht. Einige Stücke dieser Definition beziehen sich offenbar auf Tatbestände der Erfahrung: Menschen, im Verband, seßhaft, auf einem Gebiet. Ein anderes Stück aber, die ursprüngliche Herrschermacht, erweckt Zweifel. „Ursprünglich" kann nichts anderes besagen, als daß die Macht keine andere Quelle habe als den Staat selbst, daß sie nirgendwo anders hergeleitet, daß sie absolut sei. Ein Blick auf die Wirklichkeit zeigt, daß die Behauptung falsch ist. Eine absolute, eine ursprüngliche Macht ist eine Macht über allen Mächten; sie hat keine Macht neben sich oder über sich, und unter sich nur Mächte von ihren Gnaden. Die Macht des Herrschers aber

hat Schranken im Innern, denn es gibt Dinge, die keine Herrscher tun kann, ohne zu stürzen, und sie hat Schranken nach
außen an anderen Herrschermächten.

Ein Pluralismus von Mächten zwingt zur Weiterfrage nach
ihrer Abkunft. Die Ursprünglichkeit der Macht, ihre Supre-
matie, hat zum Inhalt einen Superlativ, die Behauptung, daß
die betreffende Macht die höchste sei. Für Dante verstand es
sich von selbst, daß der Pluralismus der Mächte zur Frage nach
ihrer Legitimierung und Ordnung nötigte, mit dem Ziel, die
Formel für die Einheit der vielen Mächte zu finden, und den
Supremat in das göttliche Einheitsprinzip der Machtordnung
zu verlegen. In unserer Schuldefinition bemerken wir nichts
von einer solchen Verpflichtung. Der Supremat wird schlicht
als Inhalt eines Erfahrungsurteils mit dem Anspruch auf
Richtigkeit behauptet. Die vollständig ausgegliederte Schöpfungsordnung wird durch sie gleichsam dekapitiert, das göttliche Haupt wird abgeschlagen und an die Stelle des welt-
transzendenten Gottes tritt der Staat als die letzte Bedingung
und der Ursprung seines eigenen Seins. Die wechselseitig sich
hemmende Vielzahl der Mächte treibt den Gedanken einer
umfassenden Einheit hervor — es sei denn, wir versagen uns
den Schritt des Verstandes, bleiben an dieser Stelle stehen und
glauben, daß die Welt von dämonischen Mächten bevölkert
sei, alle gleich ursprünglich, und die Frage nach der Einheit
ohne Sinn/ Die Behauptung der Ursprünglichkeit biegt aus der
Bahn des ordnenden Denkens aus; sie setzt sich über die Regeln
vernünftiger Sichtung erfahrenen Stoffes hinweg; sie ver-
weigert den rationalen Diskurs; der Geist, der sie denkt, wird
aus einem Partner des Gesprächs zu einem Faktum anderer
Ordnung, dessen Ursprüngen wir nachzugehen haben.

Die Schuldefinition läßt uns allerdings im Stich und wir
können uns nur weitertasten, indem wir zu den geschichtlichen
Quellen aufsteigen, aus denen die Behauptung entsprungen
ist. Hegel war es, der die These aufstellte, daß das Volk als

Staat der Geist in seiner unmittelbaren Wirklichkeit und daher die absolute Macht auf Erden sei. Sein mächtiger Verstand stolpert nicht über Kleinigkeiten; er zieht fest die Konsequenzen. Wenn der Staat absolute Macht ist, dann darf er im Innern keine Schranken haben. Daher gehöre zu ihm das Mechanische der Ordnung und des Dienstes, gänzlicher Gehorsam und Abtun des eigenen Meinens und Räsonierens, Abwesenheit des eigenen Geistes und zugleich intensive Gegenwart des Geistes, der im Staate aufgeht. Die Tapferkeit des einzelnen ist im Staate nicht persönlich, sondern mechanisch, nicht die einer besonderen Person, sondern eines Gliedes des Ganzen. Der Geist, der Staat geworden ist, und nicht ein Zufall, habe darum die mechanischen Mittel der Tötung erfunden, um die persönliche Gestalt der Tapferkeit in die unpersönliche zu verwandeln; die Tötungsabsicht richtet sich gegen den Feind im Abstrakten, nicht gegen eine Person.

Jetzt spüren wir schon deutlicher, was auf dem Spiele steht: es geht nicht um die Richtigkeit einer Definition, es geht um Leben und Tod; mehr noch: es geht um die Frage, ob der Mensch persönlich existieren dürfe oder sich in ein überpersönliches Realissimum aufzulösen habe. Der Kontakt von Mensch zu Mensch ist unterbrochen, un-menschliche Geistgebilde stehen einander gegenüber, und der Mensch ist gewandelt zu einem Maschinenglied, mechanisch im Getriebe mitspielend, abstrakt nach außen kämpfend und tötend. Daß die Staatsmacht ursprünglich oder absolut sei, ist nicht mehr ein Urteil des den Staat Erkennenden, sondern das Dogma eines Gläubigen. Die Existenz des Menschen verliert in seinem Erlebnis an Realität, der Staat zieht sie an sich und wird zum wahrhaft Realen, aus dem ein Wirklichkeitsstrom zurückfließt in die Menschen und sie umschaffend neu belebt als Teile des übermenschlich Wirklichen. Wir sind in das Innerste eines religiösen Erlebnisses geraten und unsere Worte beschreiben einen mystischen Prozeß.

Nach außen treten die Volksgeister, die sich in den Staaten manifestieren, in ein bestimmtes Verhältnis zueinander und zum Weltgeist. Sie stehen zu ihm als Schritte zu seiner Verwirklichung in der Geschichte in einer ähnlichen Beziehung wie die Menschen zum Staat, als dessen Maschinenteile sie funktionieren. Aufstieg und Untergang der Staaten in der Geschichte sind das Weltgericht des Geistes, vor dem jeder Volksgeist zum Tode verurteilt wird, wenn er seine Weltstunde abgedient hat. Nicht ein blindes Schicksal waltet über dem Machtkampf der Staaten, sondern in ihm legt sich die Vernunft der Welt aus. Die Schicksale der Völker, wie sie von diesen selbst als Akteuren des weltgeschichtlichen Prozesses erlebt werden, sind vor dem Dekret der Vernunft ebenso gleichgültig wie die Schicksale der Menschen vor der absoluten Macht des Staates. Vor dem Realissimum des Staates versinken die Menschen, vor dem Realissimum des Weltgeistes Volk und Staat in das unpersönliche Nichts ihrer Instrumentalität. Es wird immer die Frage bleiben, was an dieser Stelle der Hegelschen Spekulation erstaunlicher ist: der imperatorische weltordnende Verstand, der den Stoff der Geschichte in die Offenbarung des Geistes zwingt; oder der Mangel an Empfindung für das tiefe Problem der Theodizee: daß der Weltgeist, um seine Absicht zu verwirklichen, kein anderes Mittel hat als Blut und Jammer der Menschheit. Der gigantische Bau des Systems mit seiner strengen Ordnung wölbt sich über einem Abgrund von menschlichem Nihilismus, sich zehrend in Süchten nach Erfüllung mit Wirklichkeit durch ein Kollektivum.

RELIGION

Der Mensch erlebt seine Existenz als kreatürlich und darum fragwürdig. Irgendwo in der Tiefe, am Nabel der Seele, dort wo sie am Kosmos hängt, zerrt es. Dort ist der Punkt jener

Erregungen, die unzulänglich Gefühle genannt und darum leicht mit gleichnamigen oberflächlichen Bewegungen der Seele verwechselt werden. Ihre Natur ist nicht leicht zu fassen. Religiös bewegte Menschen beschreiben sie unter Bildern, die nur jene Züge treffen, die sie an ihren eigenen Erregungen erkennen. Sie sprechen vom Urgefühl, um die Tiefenschicht anzugeben, tiefer im Lebensgrund als andere Gefühle, und die ganze Existenz von diesem Grund her durchschauernd. Sie sprechen von der Unendlichkeit des Gefühls, um zu sagen, daß es sich nicht auf bestimmte Gegenstände richtet, sondern ein richtungsloses, erregtes Wogen auf dem Grunde sei. Sie nennen es ein Gefühl der schlechthinnigen Abhängigkeit, um das Erlebnis der Bindung an ein überpersönliches, übermächtiges Etwas zu zeichnen. Sie sprechen von Geworfensein und Verlassenheit, wenn die Erregungen der Existenz als einer ehemals im Schoße aufgehobenen und jetzt aus ihm entlassenen überwiegen. Sie sammeln sich aus der distentio, der Zerstreuung ihres Daseins, zurück in den Punkt ihres Ursprungs, um im Akt der intentio, der Rückspannung zu Gott, sich selbst und ihn wiederzufinden. Und das Erlebnis der Wiedervereinigung kann sich bis zu Lichterscheinungen des Göttlichen steigern. Alle die Erregungen, die dem Zustand der Kreatürlichkeit entspringen, können stimmungsmäßig verschieden gefärbt sein durch Angst, Hoffnung, Verzweiflung, Seligkeit, anschauende Ruhe, suchende Unruhe, Empörung, Auflehnung, Ergebung usw.

Der Reichtum an Schattierungen, den wir anzudeuten versuchten, entfaltet sich auf einer einzigen Dimension des religiösen Erlebnisses, an den Erregungen der Kreatürlichkeit. Er wird vervielfacht durch die Mannigfaltigkeit der Arten des Seins, in denen die Erregung sich erfüllt und erlöst. In allen Richtungen, in denen die menschliche Existenz zur Welt hin offen ist, kann das umgebende Jenseits gesucht und gefunden werden: im Leib und im Geist, im Menschen und in der Gemeinschaft, in der Natur und in Gott. Die große Zahl der grundsätzlichen Möglichkeiten und die unendliche der geschichtlich-konkreten, die sich hier auftut, verbindet sich mit den Versuchen der Selbstdeutung, mit allen Mißverständnissen und Kampfverzerrungen zu einer unerschöpflichen Fülle an Erlebnissen, ihren Rationalisierungen und Systembildungen. Dem einen stehen die Tore seiner Existenz weit offen für den Blick über die Stufen des Seins von der unbelebten Natur bis zu Gott; die Welt entfaltet sich ihm weit, ihre Inhalte treten in ein durchdachtes Verhältnis zueinander, sie schließen sich zu einer Seinsordnung, mit der Wertordnung der Seinsstufen zu einer Rangordnung, und als Antwort auf die Frage nach dem Grund des Seins zu einer Schöpfungsordnung. Ein Maximum von Aufnahme der Wirklichkeit verbindet sich mit dem Maximum an Rationalität in der Ordnung und Verknüpfung und wird gekrönt von der dogmatischen Durchbildung des geistig-religiösen Erlebnisses in einer Gottesidee, wie sie das Abendland in der analogia entis entwickelt hat. Dem andern sind nur karge Blicke in die Wirklichkeit vergönnt, vielleicht nur ein einziger: auf die Natur, einen großen Menschen, sein Volk, die Menschheit — das Gesehene wird ihm zum Realissimum, zum Allerwirklichsten, es rückt an die Stelle Gottes, und verdeckt ihm dadurch alles andere — auch, und vor allem, Gott.

Wir haben die Frage der Komplikation religiöser Grunderlebnisse durch die Typen der Realia so zugespitzt, daß die Schwierigkeiten der Erkenntnis, auf die wir einleitend hingewiesen haben, deutlich werden. Wo immer ein Wirkliches im religiösen Erlebnis sich als ein Heiliges zu erkennen gibt, wird es zum Allerwirklichsten, zum Realissimum. Diese Grundwandlung vom Natürlichen zum Göttlichen hat zur Folge eine sakrale und wertmäßige Rekristalisation der Wirklichkeit um das als göttlich Erkannte. Welten von Symbolen, Sprachzeichen und Begriffen ordnen sich um den heiligen Mittel-punkt, verfestigen sich zu Systemen, füllen sich mit dem Geist der religiösen Erregung und werden fanatisch als die „richtige" Ordnung des Seins verteidigt. Unsere Zeit ist heute dicht an dicht erfüllt von religiösen Ordnungen dieser Art, und die Folge ist eine babylonische Sprachverwirrung, da die Zeichen einer Sprache abgründig unterschiedene sakrale, magische und Wertqualitäten haben, je nach dem Sprecher, der sie gebraucht. Die Sprache ist heute innerhalb eines Volkes nicht mehr allgemein verbindlich, sondern zerrissen in Sondersprachen nach den Linien der politisch-religiösen Spaltungen. Wir verfügen nicht über selbstverständliche Worte, mit denen die geistigen Tatsachen dieses Bereiches benannt werden könnten. Anhänger von Bewegungen, die religionsfeindlich und atheistisch sein wollen, sträuben sich dagegen, daß auf dem Grund ihrer fanatischen Haltung religiöse Erlebnisse zu finden sein sollen, nur anderes als heilig verehrend als die Religion, die sie bekämpfen. Wir müssen daher eine sprachliche Entscheidung fällen: die Geistreligionen, die das Realissimum im Weltgrund finden, sollen für uns überweltliche Religionen heißen; alle anderen, die das Göttliche in Teilinhalten der Welt finden, sollen innerweltliche Religionen heißen.

Kehren wir von den Realien, von den Seinstatsachen, in denen das Göttliche erkannt wird, und von den Rekristallisationen der Wirklichkeit um das Realissimum zurück zu den Menschen, die suchen und finden. Neue Mannigfaltigkeiten von Scharfblick und Weite der Sicht, von Willens- und Gefühlsakzenten, von Geistigkeit und Triebhaftigkeit tun sich auf. Wenn das Herz empfindsam und der Geist scharf ist, genügt ein Blick in die Welt, um das Elend der Kreatur zu sehen und Wege der Erlösung zu ahnen; wenn sie unempfindlich und stumpf sind, braucht es massive Eindrücke, um schwache Empfindungen auszulösen. Der umhegte Fürstensohn sah zum erstenmal einen Bettler, einen Kranken und einen Toten — und wurde der Buddha; ein neuerer Schriftsteller sieht die Leichenhaufen und die grauenvolle Vernichtung von Tausenden in den russischen Nachkriegswirren — er kommt darauf, daß die Welt nicht in Ordnung ist, und schreibt eine Serie mäßiger Romane. Der eine sieht im Leiden das Wesen des Kreatürlichen und sucht nach der Erlösung im Weltgrund; der andere sieht es als Übelstand, dem tätig abgeholfen werden kann und soll. Manche Seele spricht stärker auf die Unzulänglichkeit der Welt an, manche auf die Seinsherrlichkeit der Schöpfung. Der eine erlebt ein Jenseits nur dann als wirklich, wenn es mit Glanz und Lärm, mit Wucht und Schrecken überlegener Macht als herrscherliche Person und Organisation auftritt; für den andern sind Antlitz und Gebärde jedes Menschen transparent und lassen seine Gotteseinsamkeit durchscheinen. Und weit spannt sich der Raum der Seelenorte, aus denen die Ekstasen aufsteigen, die Erlebnisse, in denen der Mensch sein Dasein überschreitet: von der unio mystica im Geist, über die Erhöhung im Fest der Gemeinschaft, die Hingabe an den Bund der Gefährten, das liebende Sichausweiten in die Landschaft, die Pflanzen und die Tiere, bis zu triebhaften Erschütterungen im Geschlechtsakt und im Blutrausch.

II.

ECHNATON

Die älteste politische Religion eines großen Kulturvolkes war der Sonnenglaube der Ägypter. Seine Anfänge verfließen im Dämmern der Geschichte, aber seine Entwicklung, die wir kennen bis zum Höhepunkt im Sonnenkult des Echnaton und der nachfolgenden Katastrophe, läßt die Umrisse des Problems fast deutlicher hervortreten als die späteren und genauer be-

kannten Fälle des mediterranen und europäischen Kultur-
kreises.

Die bestimmenden Faktoren des Ablaufes, in dem sich der
Mythus entfaltet, sind am Anfang der geschichtlichen Zeit
gegeben. Die Könige der ersten Dynastien verstehen sich schon
als Nachfolger des Sonnengottes Horus, eines der Herrscher
aus der Götterdynastie, die im mythischen Anfang das Land
regierte. Die vordynastischen Könige der noch getrennten
Reiche des Nordens und Südens, die als „Horusdiener" zu-
sammengefaßt werden, rücken in den Rang von Halbgöttern
und werden später in den Städten, in denen sie geherrscht haben,
als Götter verehrt. Die ersten geschichtlichen Könige führen
als Nachfolger des Horus dessen Namen als Lieblingstitel und
daneben schon den Titel eines „guten Gottes"; nach ihrem Tod
werden auch sie in ihren Tempeln als Götter verehrt. Auch die
„Staatsform der Religion" ist am Anfang der geschichtlichen
Zeit schon gegeben. Der König ist der Mittler zwischen den
Menschen und den Göttern, er allein hat theoretisch das Recht,
die Götter zu verehren, aber praktisch läßt er sich in den verschiedenen Tempeln durch Hohepriester und Priesterkollegien
in seinem Mittleramt vertreten.

Damit sind auch die Hauptfiguren des innerpolitischen
religiösen Machtkampfes vorgestellt. Es gibt zahlreiche Lokalgottheiten, deren Machtbereiche nicht immer genau gegeneinander abgegrenzt sind; es gibt nicht nur einen Sonnengott,
sondern deren mehrere in den großen Städten. Jeder Gott hat
seine Priesterschaft, und die Kollegien kämpfen untereinander
darum, das Ansehen ihres Gottes so zu steigern, daß er als
der höchste gilt. Der entscheidende Punkt im Kampf ist die
Anerkennung durch den Gottesmittler, den König; jedes der
Priesterkollegien muß sich daher bemühen, auf den König so
starken Einfluß zu gewinnen, daß ihr Gott als der dem Pharao
nächste, als der „Staatsgott" auftreten kann.

Beim Übergang von der vierten zur fünften Dynastie (etwa

2750 v. Chr.) war der Kampf der Priesterkollegien für den Sonnengott von Heliopolis, den Rê, entschieden. Schon einige Königsnamen der vierten Dynastie enthalten eine Beziehung auf den Rê; beim Übergang zur fünften zeigt sich die Priesterschaft als Königsstürzer und Königsmacher. Wahrscheinlich war der erste König der fünften Dynastie ein Oberpriester des Rê, während das Amt des Wesirs von einem Priester des Ptah ausgeübt wurde. Die Staatstheologie wurde weiter durchgebildet: der König wurde zum leiblichen Sohn des Rê, und Rê erschien jedesmal auf Erden, um der Vater des Königs zu werden. Der offizielle Königsname enthielt regelmäßig den Namen des Rê, und seit dem Ende der fünften Dynastie trat der Titel „Sohn des Rê" neben den alten Horustitel. Der Horus von Edfu war zurückgedrängt, und der Kult des Rê wurde zum Staatskult. Die politische Umwälzung, die zugleich eine religiöse ist, spiegelt sich in der Revision der Göttermythen. Alte Mythen werden umgebildet und neue treten hinzu. Rê wird zum König von Ober- und Unterägypten, der einst als irdischer König mit Toth als Wesir das Reich beherrscht hat. Die Staatstheologie folgt von jetzt ab aufs engste der politischen Entwicklung.

Eine weitere Phase des Ablaufs wird nach der Periode der inneren Wirren, die das Alte vom Mittleren Reich trennt, in der Zeit der zwölften Dynastie (2000 bis 1788) als vollendet erkennbar. Der Kult des Rê hat die Jahrhunderte überdauert, und sein Ansehen ist so gestiegen, daß viele Priesterschaften ihren jeweiligen Gott als eine Sonderform des Rê deuten, um auf diese Weise Anteil an seinem Ruhm zu gewinnen. Der politische Schwerpunkt hat sich vom nördlichen Memphis nach dem südlichen Theben verlagert, und darum wandelt sich der Gott der neuen Reichshauptstadt, der Amon von Theben, der bis dahin eine unbedeutende Lokalgottheit gewesen war, zum Amon-Rê, um der neuen politischen Bedeutung gerecht zu werden. Der Erneuerung der politischen Einheit läuft parallel die

Vereinheitlichung der Lokalgottheiten zu Gestalten des einen Sonnengottes. Ein weiterer Schritt auf dem Wege zur monotheistischen Mythenbildung ist getan.

Nach der Hyksoszeit, im Neuen Reich, folgte die Staatsreligion der neu geschaffenen straffen Militärorganisation. „Die bisher getrennt nebeneinander existierenden Priesterschaften der verschiedenen Heiligtümer wurden in einem großen Oberkollegium vereinigt, welches das ganze Land umfaßte. Das Oberhaupt des Staatstempels in Theben, der Hohepriester des Amon, stand an der Spitze dieses Kollegiums, und seine Macht wuchs dadurch über die seiner alten Rivalen in Heliopolis und Memphis weit hinaus." Der Amon von Theben war mit dem Siege des thebanischen Fürstenhauses zum höchsten Gott des Staates geworden. Die Königin wurde zur Gemahlin des Gottes, die Frau des Amon-Priesters zu seinem ersten Kebsweib.

Der neue Militärstaat griff über die Grenzen des alten ober- und unterägyptischen Reiches hinaus. Ägypten trat in die Periode des Weltreiches, und mit der territorialen Expansion, der Kenntnis neuer Länder und Völker, dem Einströmen der Beute an Gold und Sklaven, dem neuen Luxus und der Kunstblüte, der neuen politischen Gesamtlage als Weltmacht, die im regen Verkehr mit den asiatischen und den Mittelmeermächten stand, wandelte sich auch die Staatsreligion. „Wie zur Zeit der Mythenentstehung die Götter als Könige aufgefaßt wurden, die das Niltal beherrschten, weil die Sagenerzähler unter solchen Königen lebten, so hatten jetzt die Priester des Neuen Reiches, unter Königen lebend, die ein Weltreich beherrschten, in faßbarer Form eine Weltherrschaft und einen Weltplan vor sich, die Vorbedingungen zu dem Gedanken eines Weltgottes." Die Priesterschaften aller größeren Götter begannen, den Mythus ihres Gottes mit kosmologischen und demiurgischen Spekulationen zu durchdringen, aber im allgemeinen doch immer noch so, daß die Grenzen der Wirksamkeit des Gottes mit dem Nilland zusammenfielen. Nur im Falle des Sonnengottes ging die Spekulation weiter. Schon unter Amenothep III. (1405 bis 1370) war ein alter Name für die Sonne, „Aton", häufiger an Stelle des Namens des Sonnengottes gebraucht worden. Der neue Brauch des alten Namens wird bedeutend und vollendet das Werk, das mit der Vereinheitlichung der Sonnengötter als Formen des einen Rê im Mittleren Reich eingesetzt hatte: Amenothep IV. führt den Aton als den höchsten Gott ein. Zwar bestreitet er nicht seine Identität mit dem Rê, aber seine Absicht geht über den Kult der Sonne, als des sichtbaren Gottes, hinaus. Aton ist nicht die Sonnenscheibe, sondern „die Glut, die in der Sonne ist", Aton ist „der Herr der Sonne", der neue Gott ist das lebenspendende Prinzip als solches, wie es in der Wirkung der Sonne sich offenbart. Amenothep errichtet ihm einen neuen Tempel — und nun beginnt die politische Auseinandersetzung zwischen dem neuen Gott und der alten Priesterschaft, die damit endet, daß nicht nur die alten Priesterkollegien, sondern auch die alten Götter beseitigt werden. Ihre Verehrung hört auf und ihre Namen werden ausgetilgt, wo man sie auf Denkmälern findet, ja sogar der Name des Vaters des Königs, Amenotheps III., wird aus allen Tempeln Thebens ausgemerzt, weil er den Namen des Gottes Amon enthält, und schließlich änderte der König seinen eigenen Namen in Echnaton — „Es ist dem Aton angenehm". Das Werk wurde vollendet, indem der König dem Aton, dem neuen Reichsgott, an Stelle der alten Amonstadt Theben drei neue Städte in den drei Teilen des Reiches — in Ägypten, Nubien und Asien — baute; die ägyptische, Achet-Aton (das spätere Tell-Amarna), wurde die Residenz des Königs.

Der Aton übernimmt die Funktionen eines Reichsgottes, die in der Zeit, da sich das Weltreich ausdehnte, ansatzweise von den alten Göttern ausgeübt worden waren. Die Götter, welche ursprünglich nur über das Niltal herrschten, führten in der

Zeit der Eroberungskriege selbst die Truppen des Königs über
die Grenzen des alten Landes hinaus; das Vorrücken der ägyptischen Grenzsteine in Nubien und Ägypten dehnte zugleich
den Besitz des Gottes aus. Nach der Staatstheologie eroberte
der König die Welt für den Gott, und die Hilfe des Gottes
wurde erbeten, um die eroberte Welt, die Gottesherrschaft,
zu vergrößern. Da der König selbst Gott ist, gehen die göttliche
und die menschliche Sphäre ineinander über. Das menschlich
eroberte Reich und die göttlich erschaffene Welt; menschliche
und göttliche Herrschaft, menschliche und göttliche Schöpfung
lassen sich nicht genau unterscheiden. Aus diesen vorgebildeten
Ansätzen entwickelte Echnaton die Gottesidee, die wir aus
seinen Atonhymnen kennen. Aton ist durch seinen Lichtglanz
der Quell alles Lebens; er ist der Schöpfer der Menschen und
der Tiere, der Erde und des Nils, der Jahreszeiten und ihres
Wechsels. Und er krönt die Schöpfung, indem er sich offenbart
im Herzen des Echnaton. Die Hymnen lassen noch die Her-
kunft des Aton aus den Gottheiten des Niltales erkennen, in
den Versen:

> Das Dunkel wird verbannt,
> Wenn du deine Strahlen aussendest,
> Die beiden Länder feiern täglich ein Fest.

Die „beiden Länder" sind Ober- und Unterägypten. Aber
an anderer Stelle wird die Schöpfung ausgedehnt:

> Du schufst die Erde nach deinem Begehren,
> Während du allein warst,
> Die Länder Syrien und Nubien,
> Und das Land Ägypten.

Die geschaffene Erde erstreckt sich über die drei Reichs-
teile, und Ägypten wird sogar an letzter Stelle genannt. Aton
ist ein Weltgott, seine schöpferische Liebe und Fürsorge er-

streckt sich auf alles Leben, auf die ganze Erde und alle Menschen ohne Unterschied der Rasse und der Sprache:

> Du setzest jedermann an seinen Platz
> Und gibst ihnen, was sie bedürfen.
> Ein jeder hat seinen Besitz,
> Und ihre Tage sind gezählt.
> Ihre Zungen reden mancherlei Sprache,
> Auch ihre Gestalt und Farbe sind verschieden,
> Ja, du unterschiedest die Menschen.

Der Bruch mit der orthodox-ägyptischen Tradition ist sehr
scharf: Der König zeigt eine ungewöhnliche Fähigkeit, sich von
den Bindungen an eine Welt, die mit dem Nilland identisch
ist, zu befreien und die Weite der Welt in ihrer Vielgestaltig-
keit als geordnete Schöpfung zu umfassen. Er war die erste
große religiöse Individualität der Weltgeschichte.

Wie sehr nun auch die Weisheit und Seelengröße dieses
Einzigen in seiner Zeit zu bewundern ist, so bricht er doch
nicht mit der ägyptischen Staatsreligion. Der Aton ist der eine
Gott, aber er ist kein Erlöser der Menschen; er ist der Gott
des ägyptischen Weltreiches; allen ist er sorgend in ihrem
Dasein zugewandt, aber nur zu einem steigt er hinab, zum
König, der spricht:

> Du bist in meinem Herzen,
> Kein anderer ist, der dich kennt,
> Außer deinem Sohne Echnaton.

Die alte Hierarchie der sakralen Substanz bleibt erhalten.
Nur durch den Gottessohn ist die Schöpfung rückverbunden zu
dem Schöpfer, der sie aus sich entlassen hat. Nur ein einziges
Individuum der Welt lebt in unmittelbarer Beziehung zu Gott,
der Mittler, der König. Nur er weiß um den Willen des Herrn:

> Du hast mich eingeweiht in deine Pläne;

und er ist der Träger der Kraft, die sie ausführt:

> Du hast mich eingeweiht... in deine Kraft.

Sehr genau wird unterschieden zwischen den Weltzeiten und den Kraftströmen: Aton hat die Welt aus seiner Einsamkeit geschaffen:

> O du einziger Gott, dessen Macht kein anderer hat,
> Du schufst die Erde nach deinem Begehren,
> Während du allein warst. `

Die Schöpfung dauert über den ersten Akt hinaus, sie geht weiter als die dauernde Neuschöpfung der Welt im täglichen Sonnenlauf:

> Die Welt ist in deiner Hand,
> Wie du sie gemacht hast.
> Wenn du aufgegangen bist, so leben sie (sc. die Menschen),
> Gehst du unter, so sterben sie.
> Denn du selbst bist die Lebenszeit,
> Und man lebt durch dich,
> Alle Augen schauen auf deine Schönheit,
> Bis du untergehst.

Und nun schließt sich der Ring. Der Lebensstrom, der sich über die Welt ergießt, zeugt nicht sinnloses Leben, sondern sinnvolles Tun als Dienst am Aton und seinem Sohn:

> Alle Arbeit wird beiseitegelegt,
> Wenn du im Westen untergehst.
> Wenn du dich erhebst, so werden sie gemacht,

Zu wachsen für den König.
Seit du die Erde gründetest,
Hast du sie aufgerichtet für deinen Sohn,
Der aus dir selbst hervorging.

Welt und Reich sind eines, der Gottessohn ist der König,
der Strom der göttlichen Kraft schafft die Welt und erhält sie
weiter durch den Glanz der Sonne und die Befehle des Königs,
der den göttlichen Willen kennt; und von unten steigt die
Schöpfung im Dienst wieder auf zu Gott.

In den Reformen des Echnaton hat der Sonnenmythus die
Grenze seiner Entfaltung erreicht. Nach dem Tod des Königs
setzt die Reaktion ein und kehrt in wenigen Generationen
wieder zu der alten Götterverehrung zurück. Die machtvollen
Träger der Reaktion sind die verdrängten Priesterschaften
und die Militärs, die mit Grimm unter der Herrschaft des
Reformators das Reich und seine Heeresmacht verfallen sahen.
Den breiten Untergrund aber hat die Wiederherstellung dadurch, daß das Volk durch die religiöse Reform stark erregt
worden war. Wir berühren damit einen letzten wesentlichen
Punkt der Schöpfung des Echnaton, den Punkt, an dem die
Bedingungen und Grenzen der politischen Religion sichtbar
werden. Wir sagten, daß mit der Einrichtung des Atonkultes
die alten Götter beseitigt und ihre Verehrung abgebrochen
wurde. Das war, soweit es den bisherigen Staatsgott betraf,
vor allem eine Angelegenheit der Priesterschaft und der Ge-
sellschaftsschichten, die dem Staatsgott nahestanden. Es gab
jedoch in der polytheistischen Kultur Ägyptens neben der
Staatsreligion und ihren Göttern auch unpolitische Götter und
deren Kulte, wie vor allem den Osiris, seinen Kult und seine
Mysterienspiele. Der Osiris- und der Totenkult hatten sich zu
einem umfangreichen Glaubenskomplex verbunden, der die
Sittlichkeit des irdischen Lebens, das Totengericht, das Leben
nach dem Tod und die Strafe und Belohnung der Einzelseele

im Jenseits betraf; er war die Hauptreligion der unteren
Volksschichten, die in der Hierarchie der sakralen Substanz des
Sonnengottes zu entfernt standen, als daß die Staatsreligion
für ihr persönliches Leben tiefere Bedeutung hätte haben
können. Ontologisch setzte der Sonnenkult an die Probleme
von Welt und Staat, der Osiriskult an das Schicksal der Einzelseele an; religionssystematisch erlaubte der Polytheismus das
Nebeneinander der religiösen Bereiche, ohne daß sie in Konflikt gekommen wären, oder daß ein Zwang zu rationaler Konstruktion sie in ein System zusammengeschlossen hätte; gesellschaftlich stand der Sonnenkult den herrschenden Schichten
näher, der Osiriskult den beherrschten. Durch die Reform des
Echnaton wurden nun der Osiris und seine Priesterschaft ebenso kassiert wie die anderen Götter, und das durch den Polytheismus gesellschaftlich ausgewogene religiöse Leben Ägyptens empfing einen schweren Stoß. Im Bereich der politischen
Religion hatten nur Veränderungen des Personals der herrschenden Schicht stattgefunden, und die monotheistische Rationalisierung hätte sich vielleicht durchsetzen können, wenn der
König im übrigen fähig gewesen wäre, die Expansionskraft
des Staates zu erhalten. Die Volksreligion aber war vernichtet
worden, ohne daß der Atonkult für sie einen Ersatz geboten
hätte. Der Gesamtkomplex des religiösen Lebens, der im
Osiriskult enthalten war, blieb durch einen monotheistischen
Reichskult unbefriedigt. Die religionsschöpferische Leistung
des Echnaton ging über die Entwicklung des Sonnenmythus
nicht hinaus und enthielt keine Elemente der persönlichen
Ethik oder eine Lösung der persönlichen Lebens- und Todes-
frage. Der reine Staatskult mit der Hierarchie der sakralen
Substanz und der Entfernung des Untertanenlebens von Gott
war nur im polytheistischen System leistungsfähig, in dem die
anderen Wesenselemente des Menschen ihre eigene Religion
neben der politischen entfalten konnten.

III.

Wir zeichnen einige der wichtigsten sakralen Symbole, mit deren Hilfe die Verbindung des menschlich-politischen Bereiches mit dem göttlichen hergestellt wurde.

HIERARCHIE

Eine Grundform der Legitimierung der Herrschaft von Menschen über Menschen vollzieht sich im Symbol der Ausstrahlung von der göttlichen Spitze über die Hierarchie der Herrscher und Ämter bis hinunter zum letzten gehorchenden Untertan. Das Symbol hat eine weitverzweigte Geschichte, und wir verweisen nur auf einige seiner bedeutsam gewordenen Ausbildungen. Auf einem sehr hohen Grad der Vergeistigung finden wir es schon im Sonnenmythus des Echnaton, und die ägyptische Entwicklung dürfte auch für die spätere europäische nicht ohne Folgen geblieben sein. Es ist gewiß kein Zufall, daß die Sonnenbilder im Zusammenhang mit der Lehre von der Emanation göttlicher Substanz eine so entscheidende Stelle gerade bei dem Ägypter Plotin haben; und wie sehr der naturale Gestirnmythus den geistigen in der Ptolemäerzeit wieder verdrängt haben muß, ist aus dem Werk über die Monarchie des Philon von Alexandrien zu ersehen, denn er wendet sich energisch gegen den Glauben an Sonne und Mond als souveräne Götter und beharrt darauf, daß die Herrscher dem unsichtbaren Logos in der Ausübung ihres Amtes unterstellt seien. Vollkommen wurde das Bild der sakralen Ausgießung von dem Mann durchgebildet, der die gesamte ostmittelmeerische Kultur intensiv in sich aufgenommen hat, von Maimonides, und von ihm gehen die Ströme durch vielverzweigte Kanäle an das westliche Europa. Ein Jahrhundert nach Maimonides finden wir das Symbol des Ausfließens aus der Quelle, das der jüdische Denker am ägyptischen Hof mit

minutiöser Sorgfalt begründet hatte, ebenso wie das der Licht-
ausstrahlung bei Dante in seiner Monarchia: „Sonach ist es
klar, daß die Autorität des weltlichen Monarchen ohne jegliche
Vermittlung unmittelbar in der Quelle der gesamten Autorität
ihren Ursprung hat. Die Quelle, die in höchster Einfachheit
und Einheit besteht, strömt aus übergroßer Güte in viele Bäche
aus", und: der Kaiser vermag, „vom väterlichen Gnadenlichte
erleuchtet, kraftvoller auf den Erdkreis seine Strahlen zu
werfen". Das Sonnenbild wird noch einmal zum Symbol des
Monarchen durch Ludwig XIV.; in seinen Memoiren gibt er
die Gründe für die Wahl des Symbols in Formeln, die wieder
an den Hymnus des Echnaton denken lassen: „Durch seine
einzigartige Eigenschaft, durch den Glanz, der ihn umgibt,
durch das Licht, das er den anderen Sternen vermittelt, die um
ihn eine Art Hof bilden, durch die gleichmäßige und gerechte
Zuteilung des Lichtes an die Zonen der Erde, durch das Gute,
das er allerwärts schafft, indem er ohne Unterlaß überall
Leben, Freude und Tätigkeit verbreitet, durch seine unermüd-
liche Bewegung, in der er doch immer ruhig erscheint, durch
seinen stetigen und unwandelbaren Lauf, von dem er nie
abweicht und ausbiegt, ist sicherlich das Bild des Sol das leben-
digste und schönste eines großen Monarchen."

Bodin, der große Theoretiker des französischen Königtums,
hat am Ende des 16. Jahrhunderts das Symbol der sakralen
Hierarchie bis in die Einzelheiten der staatlichen und recht-
lichen Stufenordnung durchrationalisiert. Die höchste Macht
der Welt ist Gott; er ist der Seigneur der Fürsten, die unter
ihm als seine Vasallen stehen. Der Herrscher ist nicht souverän
in einem absoluten Sinn, sondern nur gegenüber den Untertanen; er selbst ist an Gott und seine Gebote ebenso gebunden
wie der Untertan an die des Herrschers. Vom Herrscher strahlt
das Befehlsrecht weiter aus über die Pyramide der Staats-
organe bis hinunter zu den Untertanen. Und umgekehrt läuft
wieder der Zug der Bindungen: „Wie die Verträge und Testa-

mente der Untertanen nicht die Ordonnanzen der Magistrate ändern können; die Edikte der Magistrate nicht die coutume; die coutume nicht die Gesetze des souveränen Fürsten, so können auch die Gesetze des souveränen Fürsten nicht die Gesetze Gottes und der Natur ändern." Die einzige Lockerung wird in das strenge System der Emanation göttlichen Willens über die Ränge der Potenzen durch den christlichen Glauben an die Gottesunmittelbarkeit des Menschen hineingetragen: der König ist nur an Gott gebunden, aber die Magistrate sind es an Gott und den König, die Untertanen an Gott („denn ihn muß man immer voranstellen"), den König und die Magistrate. In diesem Punkt, der Anerkennung der menschlichen Person in ihrer Unmittelbarkeit zu Gott, weicht die sakral-politische Hierarchie von der Symbolik des Echnaton ab, in der der Herrscher die Stelle des ausschließlichen Mittlers zwischen Gott und den Menschen hat. Im übrigen ist die Stufenordnung Bodins das Bild der inneren Staatsordnung Europas geblieben bis in die säkularisierten neueren Rechtsstufentheorien. Die staatsimmanente Hierarchie der Ämter und Normen hat sich verselbständigt und war fähig, nach der Dekapitierung Gottes sich mit jeder beliebigen legitimierenden Symbolik zu verbinden.

EKKLESIA

In der Symbolik der Hierarchie ist der Staat keine in sich geschlossene Einheit, sondern aufgelöst in die Ränge der Herrschaft, die über den irdischen Herrscher bis zu Gott reichen. Zwar droht schon hier die Person des Untertanen von Gott durch die Mittlerfunktionen der Hierarchie abgeschnitten zu werden, aber es ist, auch wenn ihre Unmittelbarkeit nicht wie bei Bodin ausdrücklich gewährt wird, doch immer noch ein einziger göttlicher Kraftstrom, der aus der Quelle sich über die Stufen der Pyramide bis zu ihrer Basis ergießt. Die Herrschaftsordnung ist sakral durchblutet, aber sie ist nicht selbst das Allerheiligste. Die Vergöttlichung der irdischen Herrschaftsordnung, ihre innerweltliche Schließung und die gleichzeitige Dekapitierung des überweltlichen Gottes, ist an eine größere Zahl von Voraussetzungen gebunden.

Die Schließung einer herrschaftlich organisierten Gemeinschaft erfordert vor allem, daß die Gemeinschaft als Einheit mit einem in ihr selbst ruhenden Existenzzentrum erlebt wird. Der naturale Ansatz für das Wachstum der partikulären, innerweltlichen, sakral-politischen Gemeinschaft ist in der Primitivperiode immer — sei es matriarchalisch oder patriarchalisch — die Abstammungsgemeinschaft. Ihre Symbolwelt ragt in zahlreichen Fragmenten in die Geschichte der Hochkulturen und bis in unsere Zeit. Die griechische Polis war noch fest auf die Stammesverbände als Kulteinheiten gegründet, und die Aufnahme in den Staatsverband konnte nur auf dem Weg über den Eintritt in den Stammeskultverband erfolgen. Daneben gab es in der griechischen — so wie in der ägyptischen Welt — wahrscheinlich unter orientalischem Einfluß die persönliche apolitische Religiosität der Mysterien. Im vollen Licht der Geschichte spielt die politisch-religiöse Tragödie des Sokrates, des Mannes, der durch die göttliche Stimme seines Daimonion und den Auftrag des Orakels von Delphi berufen war, die politisch-religiöse Reform seiner Polis durchzuführen, und an ihrem Widerstande zugrunde ging; er weigerte sich zu fliehen, weil eine Existenz außerhalb der sakralen Gemeinschaft für ihn sinnlos war. Ein neuerer Historiker hat an ihm, wie an Platon und Aristoteles, eine gegenüber dem christlichen Alter noch geringer entwickelte Stufe der Geistigkeit festgestellt, weil es diesen Denkern noch nicht möglich war, die Schranken der sakral-politischen innerweltlichen Gemeinschaft zu durchbrechen und die Möglichkeit der gottesunmittelbaren religiösen Existenz zu erkennen.

Weit stärker und deutlicher als durch die Reste der stamm-

staatlichen Gemeinschaftssymbolik sind die modernen innerweltlichen politischen Einheiten durch die Umbildungen der
Ekklesia-Substanz bestimmt. Die christliche Idee, wie sie in
den Paulusbriefen und dem nahestehenden Ebräerbrief entwickelt wird, versteht die Ekklesia, die Gemeinde als den
mystischen Leib Christi. In mehreren Abwandlungen wird die
organische Analogie durchgebildet. Einmal sind die Ämter
der Ekklesia aufeinander hingeordnet wie die Glieder eines
Leibes und ergänzen sich zur Einheit des irdischen Leibes,
dessen Pneuma Christus ist; ein anderes Mal wird das Leib-
gleichnis über die irdischen sichtbaren Glieder des Leibes hinaus erstreckt bis zu Christus selbst, der zum Haupt des Leibes
wird; umgekehrt kann wieder der geistige Gehalt überwiegen
und das Pneuma Christi gießt sich kraft seines Pleroma, seiner
Fülle in die irdischen Glieder aus, so daß die Personalität des
Erlöserpneumas fast aufgehoben wird; unterstützt wird die
Analogie durch Reste der Abstammungssymbolik in der Idee
des Christus als des zweiten Adam, des zweiten Stammvaters
der Menschheit, und die den Mysterienkulten nahestehende
Form des Abendmahls. — Die paulinischen Schwankungen
zeichnen die Möglichkeiten der Weiterbildung vor. Die Charismata, die dem Pneuma Christi entströmen und den Gliedern
des Leibes ihre Funktion verleihen, können sich über das von
Paulus entworfene Schema der Ränge der Urgemeinde erweitern und um die politisch-herrscherlichen Funktionen ergänzen. Die Herrscherfunktion bekommt dadurch ihren Status
im corpus mysticum und ist artmäßig nicht mehr von den
Priester- und Lehrfunktionen unterschieden. Es gibt keine
Grenze zwischen dem politischen und dem religiösen Bereich;
das corpus mysticum ist eine in sich gegliederte Einheit, in dem
es ein Sakrament der Königssalbung neben dem Sakrament
der Priesterweihe gibt; die Ausübung des Königsamtes ist eine
sakrale Funktion neben anderen. Geschichtlich hat sich diese
Möglichkeit etwa im sacrum imperium des 9. Jahrhunderts

verwirklicht. Andere Gestaltungen knüpfen an die Möglichkeit an, unter den Ämtern des corpus mysticum eine Hierarchie zu entwickeln, so daß eines der Ämter das höchste wird und die anderen nur durch seine Vermittlung in das Korpus und seine Charismata eingegliedert sind, wie in der Idee des päpstlichen Supremates über den Herrscher. Anderseits wieder kann die Gottesunmittelbarkeit der Funktionen zum Prinzip erhoben werden wie in der Kaiseridee Dantes. Und grundsätzlich kann das Symbol einer durch das Pneuma Christi konstituierten Gemeinschaft sich zu innerweltlichen Körpern umbilden, wenn die einmal Wirklichkeit gewordene geistige Einheit sich wieder mit naturalen Gehalten auffüllt. Die Möglichkeit der Auffüllung deutet sich schon in den frühchristlichen Jahrhunderten an, wenn die Ekklesia der Christen als populus Christianus zum Volk unter Völkern wird. Die geschichtlichen Quellen der späteren Umbildung waren das antike Kaisertum des Gottmenschen und die Bindung des Herrschers an das Volk durch die acclamatio des populus Romanus, und die germanischen Stammes- und Königsideen.

Die von Christus konstituierte Ekklesia hat sich mannigfach gewandelt; durch alle Wandlungen hindurch aber bleibt das Grundgerüst, auf das es uns ankommt, erkennbar. Von ihr stammen in gerader Linie die christlichen Kirchen, aber die Idee ist nach gewissen ihrer Teile auch in den staatlichen Gemeinschaften lebendig geblieben. Im Kontinuum der Ekklesia stehen wir überall dort, wo die innerweltlich gewordenen partikulären Gemeinschaften die Gleichheit und Brüderlichkeit aller Glieder der Gemeinschaft anerkennen, und zwar auch dort, wo sich die Gemeinschaften und Bewegungen scharf antikirchlich und antichristlich einstellen bis zur Einführung einer neuen Staatsreligion, wie in der französischen Revolution. Das Fortbestehen der christlichen Liebesgemeinschaft im französischen Solidarismus wird von den laizistischen Denkern der Dritten Republik anerkannt und die Idee der Solidarität als

die säkularisierte christliche Karitas gedeutet. Die paulinische
Idee der Ausgliederung des corpus mysticum in die sich ergän-
zenden Funktionen der Gemeinschaft spielt mit in den Arbeits-
teilungstheorien der englischen und französischen Ökonomen
und Soziologen. Die starke ekklesiastische Durchsetzung der
amerikanischen nationalen Gemeinschaft ist bekannt; infolge
der Tradition des Puritanismus sind die Ideen weit weniger
verändert worden, und wir finden eine paulinische Kategorie
wie die „likemindedness", die Gleichgeistigkeit der Glieder des
Körpers, als soziologischen Grundbegriff in der Wissenschaft
ausgebildet. Hier ist auch, infolge der besonderen sozial-
geschichtlichen Lage der Vereinigten Staaten, die Gleichheits-
idee schärfer durchgebildet worden zu der Idee, daß nur die
wirklich Gleichen im Geiste Vollglieder der Gemeinschaft sein
können; die innerweltliche Ekklesia reagiert mit besonderer
Empfindlichkeit auf die Bedrohung ihres die Gemeinschaft der
Gleichen konstituierenden Geistes und hat in der Erziehungs-
psychologie und der Assimilationsanstrengung die Mittel geschaffen, um die heterogenen Elemente, die in der Einwan-
derungszeit das naturale Korpus aufbauten, in ein spirituales
Korpus einzugliedern. Und auch dort, wo die innerweltliche
Ekklesia sich religiös-inhaltlich in scharfer Auseinandersetzung
mit der christlichen Ekklesia befindet, wie im deutschen Nationalsozialismus, lebt in der Forderung der spirituellen Konfor-
mität die Grundform des mystischen, durch das Pneuma zur
Einheit gebundenen Korpus weiter, ebenso wie die christliche
Karitas in den säkularisierten Formen der Hilfswerke für die
armen Volksgenossen.

SPIRITUAL UND TEMPORAL

Einer der wichtigsten Faktoren in der Bildung der innerweltlichen Gemeinschaften war die Spaltung der Ekklesia nach

3*

den Linien von spiritual und temporal. Der Gegensatz erfüllt sich geschichtlich mit mehr als einem Inhaltspaar, und wir können nur zwei oder drei Haupttypen herausgreifen.

Die erste große geschichtsphilosophische Interpretation des Problems hat Augustin gegeben. Die Weltgeschichte ist die gewaltige Auseinandersetzung zwischen der himmlischen und der irdischen Civitas, dem Reiche Christi und dem Reiche des Bösen. Die beiden Reiche sind nicht institutionell zu fassen, etwa als Kirche und Staat (wenngleich sich bei Augustinus gelegentlich die Tendenz findet, den Staat als das magnum latrocinium zu verstehen), sondern als Gemeinschaften der Gefolgschaft Christi und seiner Feinde. Die civitas terrena spaltet sich von der civitas Dei durch den Abfall der bösen Engel ab; die civitas Dei beginnt als Engelsstaat und endet als Königreich Gottes, ihre Bürger sind alle rechtschaffen nach Gott Lebenden. Die Kirche ist die Repräsentantin des Gottesstaates auf Erden, aber zu ihren sakramental verbundenen Gliedern gehören auch Bürger der civitas terrena, und außerhalb der Kirche gibt es Bürger der civitas Dei. Die Entwicklung der Symbole hat in einer Kampfzeit des Christentums stattgefunden, aus Anlaß der Eroberung Roms durch die Westgoten (410), und richtet sich gegen den die Kirche gefährdenden Gedanken, daß das Christentum, die junge Staatsreligion des römischen Reiches, den Staat nicht gegen das Unglück geschützt habe. Um dieser gefährlich öffentlichen Meinung klarzumachen, daß das Christentum nicht eine Lebens- und Unfallversicherung sei, entwickelt Augustin das Bild der echten christlichen Haltung und des Sinnes der Gefolgschaft Christi. Systematisch ist die große Konzeption sehr verwickelt und nicht völlig geschlossen; sie läßt allerwärts die künftige Problematik durchblicken. Die civitas Dei ist weder identisch mit der Kirche, noch mit dem Weltalter, das mit der Erlösungstat Christi angebrochen ist, noch mit dem ewigen Sabbat des göttlichen Endreiches. Sie umfaßt sie alle ganz oder zum Teil und dazu noch die vorchristliche Gottesgefolgschaft; sie ist bis zum äußersten mit den Spannungen geladen, die sich daraus ergeben, daß die kirchlich-institutionellen Elemente mit den apokalyptischen der neuen Weltzeit und den eschatologischen des Endreiches in eine Einheit zusammengezwungen werden. Es ergibt sich die Vielzahl der Dualismen, von Sakramentsgemeinschaft der Kirche und Umwelt, irdisch-diesseitiger und spirituell-jenseitiger Zugehörigkeit zur civitas Dei, von Gottesreich und Teufelsreich. Und schließlich hat die institutionelle Staatswirklichkeit und die Idee, daß zum Glück der Welt die Reiche am besten zahlreich und klein wären, ähnlich wie eine Stadt sich aus zahlreichen Bürgerfamilien zusammensetzt, eine nicht völlig klare Stelle im System. Die Spannung des Systems spiegelt die Spannung des Kampfes, in dem das Christentum steht. Es gibt noch keine reduzierten Schemata des Gegensatzes von geistlicher und weltlicher Gewalt in den Institutionen von Kirche und Staat, und von diesseitigem und jenseitigem persönlichen Leben. Dafür gibt es harte, lebensverachtende Formeln, wenn Augustinus sich gegen die Klagen über das römische Massaker wendet: „Viele gingen auf allerlei gräßliche Art zugrunde. Wenn man dies beklagen muß, so ist es doch das gemeinsame Los aller, die zu diesem Leben geboren werden. Soviel weiß ich, daß keiner gestorben ist, der nicht ohnehin einmal hätte sterben müssen." Formeln dieser Art finden sich heute in den politisch-religiösen Gemeinschaften wieder, so wenn Ernst Jünger gegen das Grauen der Lebensvernichtung im Kriege sagt, der Tod sei bitter, wann immer er trifft — eine Härte, die sich legitimiert im Glauben: „Die Gefallenen gingen, indem sie fielen, aus einer unvollkommenen in eine vollkommene Wirklichkeit, aus dem Deutschland der zeitlichen Erscheinung in das ewige Deutschland ein."

Enger und schärfer zeichnet sich das Problem auf der Höhe der Scholastik ab, als die Bruchlinien des sacrum imperium schon sichtbar sind, in der Staatslehre des Thomas von Aquino.

Die Ämter innerhalb der großen Ekklesia haben sich verfestigt und gegeneinander verselbständigt. Die Reichsauflösung durch die Bildung der großen Feudalorganisationen hat begonnen; als erster „Staat im Reich" entsteht die Feudalkirche, ihr folgen in der institutionellen Durchbildung die Fürsten, als erster und am radikalsten Friedrich II. im sizilischen Staat. Die Rezeption der aristotelischen Staatslehre ermöglicht es Thomas, das Verhältnis der kirchlichen zur fürstlichen Funktion zu bestimmen. In den Inhalten der Politik folgend, weist Thomas dem Fürsten die Aufgabe zu, die weltliche Herrschaft über seine Untertanen so auszuüben, daß ihre materielle und geistige Existenz sie optimal befähigt, ihr Seelenheil zu verfolgen; die spirituelle Sorge ist Sache der Kirche. Gemäß dem höheren Rang des spiritualen Zweckes über dem temporalen ist die fürstliche Funktion der kirchlichen im Rang untergeordnet. Die Tragweite und die Schranken der Idee werden sichtbar beim Vergleich mit Aristoteles selbst. Der griechische Denker bewegt sich noch im politisch-religiösen System der Polis. Der Sinn des persönlichen und des staatlichen Lebens werden analogisch verstanden und die Analogie über Mensch und Staat zu Welt und Gott erweitert. Das wertvollste Leben ist das Leben der Tätigkeit im Geiste, denn als geistig Tätiger ist der Mensch am meisten sich selbst genug, bedarf er am wenigsten äußerer Mittel, und ist also Gott, dem in sich selbst ruhenden und sich selbst genügenden, am ähnlichsten. Und ebenso ist der autarke, in sich selbst lebende, nicht allzusehr in Beziehungen zu anderen verflochtene Staat der beste, weil sein Leben in sich selbst das Analogon göttlich-kosmischen Seins ist. Diese Endstufe einer vergeistigten Polisreligion ist in sich vollendet. Die Übertragung in das thomistische System läßt weite Stoffbereiche der aristotelischen Politik bestehen, aber sie zerstört ihren zentralen Sinn. Der Kosmos des gottanalogen Staates wird aufgebrochen; die persönliche und gemeinschaftliche Existenz wird in zwei Reiche zerlegt und der politisch-temporale Bereich durch den spiritualen überhöht. Das Problem der Staatsinstitution, das bei Augustin als unwichtig an die Wand gedrückt war, rückt jetzt in die Mitte, und es ist deutlich nur mehr eine Frage der geschichtlichen Situation, wann die Staatsinstitution sich von ihrer Unterordnung unter die Feudalkirche trennt und selbst die sakralen Gehalte an sich zieht. Friedrich II. hatte diesen Schritt schon getan. Nach der Eroberung Jerusalems und der Selbsterhöhung zum Messiaskönig spricht der Kaiser als Autokrator, als heidnischer Gottmensch. Die antike Justitia wird zur Staatstugend erklärt, ihr Kult zur Staatsreligion, das Volk zum Dienst gezwungen, das Triumphtor von Kapua als Altar errichtet. Der Papst erklärt den Kaiser zum Antichrist. Die erste innerweltliche politische Religion auf dem Boden der christlichen Ekklesia war entstanden.

APOKALYPSE

Wir haben bisher aus der Gliederung der Ekklesia und ihrer Geschichte einzelne charakteristische Phasen herausgegriffen, um an ihnen zu zeigen, wie die politisch-religiöse Bildwelt sich aufbaut und als Grundgerüst der europäischen Entwicklung bis in die Gegenwart erkennbar bleibt. Die Geschichte wurde dabei von außen gesehen, als eine Folge von Abwandlungen einer religiösen Symbolwelt. Wir wenden uns nun zu einer neuen Symboldimension, zu den Ausdeutungen der Entwicklung von innen, von den beteiligten Menschen und Mächten her.

Das Grundschema der religiösen Geschichtsdeutung ist schon in der paulinischen Gliederung der Weltgeschichte in die drei Reiche der heidnischen lex naturalis, der lex mosaica des Alten Testamentes und des dritten, des christlichen Reiches, enthalten. Von diesem Anfang entwickelt sich die Deutung weiter, indem sie jeweils die historischen Stoffe, die für die Zeit wichtig sind, aufnimmt, bis zum Höhepunkt im deutschen Symbolismus des 12. Jahrhunderts und der Verkündigung des dritten Reiches in dem Jahrhundert von Joachim von Floris bis zu Dante. Die Geschichtsdeutung ist symbolisch, insofern die Stoffe geordnet und gedeutet werden als Ausdruck des göttlichen Willens in der Geschichte. Das rationale Schema der Ordnung sind die heiligen Zahlen: die Dreizahl der Trinität, die Siebenzahl der Gaben des Heiligen Geistes, das Hexameron, das Sechstagewerk, die alttestamentlichen Geschlechterzahlen der 42 von Abraham bis Christus, und die Hälfte dieser Zahl in den 21 Generationen vor Abraham. Die erste große christliche Geschichtsphilosophie, die mit den Mitteln der Symbolik arbeitet, die augustinische, wurde schon gestreift: das Zeitalter Christi ist das sechste und zugleich letzte irdische, als siebentes folgt das selige jenseitige Endreich. In der Blüte des deutschen Symbolismus im 12. Jahrhundert wird die Methode vollendet, um dann bei Joachim von Floris jene Wandlung zu erfahren, die von entscheidender Bedeutung für die Dynamik der Ekklesia und ihrer innerweltlichen Abspaltungen geworden ist. Joachim hat die Formel für eine Seelen- und Denkrichtung gefunden, die schon länger zur Öffentlichkeit und Geltung drängte, nach der das Reich Christi nicht, wie in der älteren Einteilung, das letzte irdische Reich ist, sondern ihm noch ein drittes zu folgen hat. Das erste ist in dieser Zählung das göttliche des Alten Bundes, das zweite das christliche, das dritte das der dritten göttlichen Person, des Heiligen Geistes, das zusammenfällt mit dem siebenten Weltalter, worauf erst der ewige Sabbat des Endreiches folgt. Jedes der Reiche ist in sich in sieben Zeitalter gegliedert, und diese Zeiten des vorchristlichen wie des christlichen Reiches, für die der geschichtliche Stoff vorliegt, sind symbolisch bestimmt durch ihre Führer. Am Anfang des zweiten Reiches steht, nach den Vorläufern Zacharias und Johannes, Christus; am Anfang des dritten Reiches, das nahe bevorsteht, eine Erscheinung, die schlechthin DUX, der Führer, genannt wird. Den Anbruch des dritten Reiches berechnet Joachim für 1200, die joachitischen Franziskanerspiritualen berechnen ihn für 1260. Die geschichtlichen Modelle, an denen die Apokalypse des dritten Reiches ihre Stütze fand, waren die Ordensgründungen, die neuen religiones, in denen die ansteigende Entwicklung des vollkommenen Lebens im Heiligen Geist sichtbar wurde. Die Offenbarung verdichtet sich in den ersten Franziskanergenerationen zu der Auffassung des Franz von Assisi als des verkündigten Dux und des Joachim und Dominikus als der Vorläufer, das Werk Joachims wird erkannt als das evangelium aeternum der Apokalypse (14,6). Das dritte Reich Joachims ist nicht eine neue Institution, die revolutionär an die Stelle der Kirche zu treten hätte, sondern ein Prozeß der Vergeistigung der Ekklesia und der Umbildung der Weltkirche zu einem neuen Orden kontemplativen vergeistigten Mönchstums; im Gegensatz zu der Reichsapokalypse des Paulus enthält die Offenbarung des Joachim daher auch keine Hinweise auf die Sozialordnung des dritten Reiches; im Reich der spiritualis intellegentia leben die Menschen kontemplativ, nicht mehr aktiv-kontemplativ wie der Klerus der Weltkirche, sie leben geistig und arm, brüderlich, alle vom gleichen Rang, ohne Zwangsordnung.

Die christliche Reichsapokalypse und der Symbolismus des Spätmittelalters bilden den geschichtstiefen Untergrund der apokalyptischen Dynamik in den modernen politischen Religionen. Die christliche Ordensbewegung seit Benedikt und vor allem die Bewegung der Bettelorden, die Gründung neuer religiones innerhalb des Christentums, hat die seelische Haltung der Erneuerung des Geistes und der Mitarbeit an der Vervollkommnung des christlichen Existenzideals als eines diesseitigen erzeugt. Die ansteigende Linie der Vollkommenheit geistigen Seins ist zu einem der stärksten Elemente der innerweltlichen Dynamik seit der Renaissance geworden, im

Glauben an die perfectibilitas der menschlichen Vernunft, an die unendliche Höherentwicklung der Menschheit zum idealen Endzustand in der Aufklärung, in den deistischen Ordensgründungen der Maçonnerie zur Vervollkommnung des Weltbaues, und im Fortschrittsglauben als der Volksreligion des 19. Jahrhunderts. Der Symbolismus der Reichsapokalypse lebt fort im Symbolismus des 19. und 20. Jahrhunderts, in den drei Reichen der Marx-Engels'schen Geschichtsphilosophie, im dritten Reich des Nationalsozialismus, im faschistischen dritten Rom, nach dem antiken und dem christlichen. Auch die inhaltlichen Bestimmungen des dritten Reiches sind erhalten geblieben: und zwar der Glaube an die Auflösung der weltkirchlichen Institution durch die Vergeistigung zu Orden des vollkommenen Lebens im Heiligen Geist im Glauben an des Absterben des Staates und die brüderliche freie Assoziation der Menschen im kommunistischen dritten Reich; der Glaube an den Bringer des Reiches, Dantes fünfhundert, fünf und zehn (DVX), in den Führerfiguren und -mythen unserer Zeit; die Orden des neuen Reiches in den kommunistischen, faschistischen und nationalsozialistischen Bünden und Eliten als dem Kern der neuen Reichsorganisationen.

IV.

DER LEVIATHAN

Der Prozeß, in dem sich die abendländische Ekklesia in die staatlichen Teilgemeinschaften auflöst, durchzieht das Mittelalter und erreicht in der Zeit des Absolutismus mit der organisatorischen Abschließung der Staaten gegeneinander einen deutlichen Einschnitt. Nicht alle Gebiete Europas erreichen diesen Punkt gleichzeitig: die westlichen Nationalstaaten waren die Träger der Entwicklung und sind bis heute die großen Prototypen geblieben. In ihnen wurde auch zuerst die Theologie der neuen Ekklesia durchdacht, als partikulärer Gemeinschaft neben anderen, weltlich-politisch und sakral in so inniger Durchdringung, Staat und Kirche in so enger Einheit, daß die Gegensätze von temporal und spiritual sinnlos werden.

Der große Theologe der partikulären gottesunmittelbaren Ekklesia war Hobbes. Er wird oft als Theoretiker der absoluten Monarchie verstanden; er war auch das, aber er war mehr, denn er hat das Symbol des Leviathan geschaffen, des unmittelbar unter Gott stehenden und im göttlichen Auftrag gegenüber den Untertanen omnipotenten Staates*). Die Konstruktion des Symbols vollzieht sich in zwei Stufen, zuerst einer naturalen Konstruktion der Staatsperson, die für alle Zeiten verbindlich sein will, und dann in der Konstruktion der naturalen Einheit als einer christlichen Ekklesia am geschichtlichen Ort des 17. Jahrhunderts./Um die neue naturale Einheit der politischen Nation aufzubauen, bedient sich Hobbes aus Gründen der biblischen Überlieferung des Alten Bundes einer Vertragstheorie. Die Menschen sollen sich im Naturzustand durch einen Vertrag gegenseitig verpflichtet haben, durch Stimmenmehrheit einen Souverän über sich zu setzen und ihm alle Gewalt zu übertragen. Man hat Hobbes wegen dieser Konstruktion einen Vertragstheoretiker genannt — das ist nicht falsch, aber es betrifft nur ein traditions- und zeitgebundenes Instrument seiner Theorie, nicht deren Wesen. Das Wesentliche ist

---

*) Das Bild des Leviathans hat Hobbes der Bibel entnommen. In Hiob cap. 40 und 41 wird das Ungeheuer beschrieben: „Sein Herz ist so kalt wie ein Stein und so fest wie ein Stück vom untersten Mühlstein. Wenn er sich erhebt, so entsetzen sich die Starken, und wenn er daher bricht, so ist keine Gnade da." „Auf Erden ist ihm niemand zu gleichen; er ist gemacht, ohne Furcht zu sein. Er verachtet alles, was hoch ist; er ist ein König über alle Stolzen."

aus den Formeln für das Ergebnis des Vertrages zu erschließen:
die vorher gestaltlose Vielzahl von Menschen wählt sich nicht
einen Herrscher, sondern verbindet ihre Vielheit zu der Einheit einer Person; die Vielzahl wird zur Einheit des Commonwealth, indem sie sich einen Persönlichkeitsträger verschafft; das
Commonwealth, nicht der gewählte Souverän, ist die Person, die
von jetzt ab als Akteur der Geschichte auftritt. Wir sagten schon,
daß die wichtigste Voraussetzung für die Entstehung der innerweltlichen Gemeinschaftsreligion das Selbstverständnis einer
Gemeinschaft als in sich zentrierter Einheit sei. Das Leviathansymbol des Hobbes tut einen entscheidenden Schritt in dieser
Richtung; es erreicht zwar nicht die kugelhafte kosmos-analoge
Geschlossenheit des aristotelischen Polissymbols, aber die
offene Gliederung der christlichen Ekklesia ist zum größten
Teil aufgehoben. Zwar geht noch die Hierarchie bis zu Gott
und das Commonwealth entsteht gemäß dem Auftrag Gottes,
aber von Gott geht die Hierarchie nach unten nicht mehr zu
Personen, welche die Ränge der Ekklesia besetzt halten, sondern zu der Gemeinschaft als einer Kollektivperson; sie geht
zum Souverän nicht als dem Herrscher über Untertanen, sondern als dem Persönlichkeitsträger des Commonwealth. Wenn
man geschichtliche Vergleiche ziehen will, dann müßte man
Hobbes für die partikuläre innerweltliche Ekklesia eine ähn-
liche Stelle zuerkennen wie Paulus für die Symbolschöpfung
der christlichen Gemeinschaft. Die neue Gemeinschaft gewinnt
ihre Einheit durch den Souverän in der gleichen symbolisch-
mystischen Weise wie die paulinische Ekklesia durch Pneuma
und Kephale des Christus. Das weltliche Substrat des Commonwealth sind die partikulären Nationen, aber ihre Einheit ist
ein corpus mysticum wie das christliche. Die einzige Parallele
zu diesem Prozeß bieten innerhalb der europäischen Entwicklung im engeren Sinne die Germanengeschichten der Völker-
wanderungszeit. Dort finden wir, so wie bei Hobbes, die Krea-
tion der Person eines Stammes durch die Setzung eines Königs

und den Verlust der Person durch seinen Tod. Die Verbindung von rex und gens ist so eng, daß Setzung oder Verlust des Königs den Gewinn oder Verlust der geschichtlich unmittelbaren Existenz des nationalen Wesens bedeuten. Im gleichen Sinne schafft der Herrschervertrag des Hobbes den Staat als geschichtliche Person, als den „Mortal God", den irdischen Gott, dem die Menschen nächst dem „Immortal God", dem ewigen Gott, Frieden und Sicherheit verdanken.

Das Commonwealth ist nicht nur als Kosmos politischer Macht geschlossen, sondern auch geistig, denn der Souverän, sei er ein Monarch oder eine Versammlung, hat das Recht, zu beurteilen, welche Meinungen und Lehren geeignet sind, die Einheit des Commonwealth zu wahren und zu fördern; er hat zu entscheiden, welche Menschen und inwiefern sie in Versammlungen sprechen dürfen, und er hat die Vorzensur über Druckwerke auszuüben. Die Begründung könnte von einem modernen Propagandaminister geschrieben sein: die Handlungen der Menschen werden durch ihre Meinungen bestimmt, und wer die Meinungen richtig lenkt, der lenkt die Handlungen zu Frieden und Eintracht; zwar müssen die Lehren wahr sein, aber ein Konflikt könne nicht entstehen, denn Lehren, die den Frieden der Gemeinschaft stören, sind nicht wahr.

So weit ist der Leviathan ein heidnisch-sakrales Symbol — um es zu einem christlichen zu machen, bedarf es der Auseinandersetzung mit dem bisherigen Symbol der christlichen Ekklesia und der Unterscheidung von ihm. Die hochscholastische Konstruktion des Thomas, in der die temporale der spiritualen Ordnung im Rang unterstellt und von ihr organisatorisch unterschieden war, bricht jetzt auseinander; die weltliche Ordnung füllt sich mit den nationalen Gehalten zu einer eigenpersönlichen Einheit. Die Polemik des Hobbes richtet sich daher gegen das Fragment des Sacrum Imperium, das noch den Anspruch auf personale Repräsentation der Christenheit und den spiritualen Vorrang erhebt, gegen die katholische Kirche. Er verwendet seine Theorie des Commonwealth, um zu beweisen, daß die Kirche kein Commonwealth sei und nicht Persönlichkeit habe, daß also die neue Ekklesia nicht Teil eines umfassenden Reiches Gottes sein könne, sondern als Einzelperson gottesunmittelbar sei. Die paulinische Reichsidee, die — um das Königscharisma ergänzt — das 9. Jahrhundert beherrscht und nach der Papst, Kaiser, König, Klerus und Laien die Glieder einer Ekklesia sind, wird energisch abgelehnt, weil sie zu der absurden Konsequenz führen würde, daß unbezweifelten geschichtlichen Gemeinschaftspersonen wie Frankreich, Spanien, Venedig dieser Charakter aberkannt und sie zu Gliedern der Ekklesia ohne gottesunmittelbaren Persönlichkeitsstatus gemacht würden. Jedes Commonwealth sei für sich eine christliche Ekklesia, wenn sein Souverän Bibel und Christentum durch Staatsgesetz verbindlich macht; der Staat sei dann zugleich Kirche, mit dem Souverän als Kirchenhaupt, unmittelbar unter Gott, ohne Vermittlung des Vicarius Christi. Ein spirituales Commonwealth als Kirche, die nicht Staat ist, sei widersinnig; die Unterscheidung von spiritual und temporal sei nur in die Welt gesetzt worden, um die Menschen zu verwirren, die Untertanen ihrem Souverän abspenstig zu machen und den Frieden der Commonwealth-Kirche zu stören.

Hobbes stützt sein Symbol durch die Rückbeziehung auf die Geschichte des Alten und des Neuen Bundes. Mit voller Wucht strömt in die englische Reformationswelt die religiöse Potenz der jüdischen Theokratie ein, um sich mit dem nationalen Bewußtsein im Symbol der sakralen Gemeinschaftsperson zu vereinigen. Sorgfältig werden die Stadien der jüdischen Geschichte verfolgt vom Bund des Abraham und der Unterwerfung Israels unter Gott über die Führerschaft Moses' und seiner Nachfolger bis zur Krisis des Abfalls, da Israel Gott als Herrn aufgibt, um einen König zu haben wie die anderen Völker. Am Beispiel Abrahams wird das Bild des geistlichen Staatsoberhauptes entwickelt. Zu Abraham allein habe Gott unmittelbar gesprochen als dem Persönlichkeitsträger seines Volkes, und darum habe im Commonwealth sich jeder Untertan, als einer, dem sich Gott nicht unmittelbar geoffenbart hat, dem Gesetz des Souveräns in allen äußeren Religionsakten und -bekenntnissen zu unterwerfen. Nur im Fühlen und Denken, das nicht nach außen in Erscheinung tritt und vom menschlichen Herrscher nicht gekannt werden kann, sei der Untertan frei und nur Gott unterworfen.

Der Souverän des christlichen Commonwealth habe die gleiche Stellung wie Abraham zu seiner Familie; nur zu ihm spricht Gott, er allein kennt seinen Willen, und er allein ist berechtigt, Wort und Willen Gottes zu interpretieren. Nach dem Vorbild der jüdisch-theokratischen Idee gewinnt das Symbol des Leviathan Züge, die denen der Reichsreligion des Echnaton verwandt sind. Wieder wird der Herrscher zum Gottesmittler; ihm allein offenbart sich Gott; er allein vermittelt den Willen Gottes an das Volk — mit dem einzigen Reservat, daß im privaten Seelenleben ein Rest von gottesunmittelbarer Personalität des Menschen erhalten bleibt.

Die Erscheinung Christi habe an der Situation nichts geändert; ihr Zweck war die Erneuerung des Bundes mit Gott, der in der Rebellion durch die Königswahl Sauls gebrochen worden war. Christus sei gesandt worden, um die Menschen von der Sünde der Rebellion zu erlösen und sie zum Reich Gottes zurückzuführen; dieses Reich aber sei ein Reich der Gnade und nicht von dieser Welt; die Königsherrschaft wird Christus erst nach der Auferstehung ausüben. Die ekklesiastische Gewalt in dieser Welt ging von Christus auf die Apostel, von diesen auf die Nachfolger durch Handauflegen über, bis Souveräne das Christentum annahmen, indem sie sich — nicht den Aposteln, sondern — Gott unmittelbar als dem offenbarten unterwarfen. Die christlichen Herrscher sind die Inhaber der ekklesiastischen Gewalt, und durch ihre Vermittlung wird die Gottesherrschaft in dieser Welt über die ihnen unterworfenen Ekklesiae wiederhergestellt.

Die neue Ekklesia steht im Kampf mit der alten christlichen und hat sich als gottgewollte gegen Ansprüche durchzusetzen, die nur als Teufelswerk verstanden werden können. Dem Symbol des Leviathan muß Hobbes daher das Symbol des Teufelsreiches entgegensetzen. Soweit die christliche Menschheit in Frage kommt, zerfällt sie in die Ekklesiae der christlichen politischen Gemeinschaften; der Versuch, eine universale christliche Ekklesia als Institution mit Persönlichkeit zu erhalten oder zu schaffen, wird als Werk des Satans verstanden; die katholische Kirche mit ihrem Anspruch auf spirituelle Hoheit über alle Christen sei das Reich der Finsternis, das die geradlinige Fortsetzung der Idee des Gottesvolkes von der jüdischen Vor-Königszeit in die Zeit des christlichen Commonwealth stören wolle. Der Staat ist die Kirche, und wer als Gegner dieser neuen Ekklesia, des Leviathan, auftritt, ist der Satan — so wie in der jüdischen Geschichte Palästina das Königreich Gottes und die benachbarten feindlichen Nationen das Reich des Erzfeindes, des Teufels, waren.

Der Gegensatz hat sich in England sehr lange erhalten. Defoe hat eine umfangreiche politische Geschichte des Teufels geschrieben; und noch 1851 hat Kardinal Newman es für nötig gehalten, die Unsinnigkeit der satanischen Deutung der katholischen Kirche darzutun, indem er auf Grund von Sätzen aus Blackstones Kommentar zur englischen Verfassung ein Bild des englischen Staates als des Teufelsreiches entwarf, das den Teufelsbildern der antikatholischen Literatur entsprach, um zu zeigen, daß dieses Verfahren beliebig angewendet werden könne. Die Satire des Kardinals ist von der Wirklichkeit überboten worden: das Teufelssymbol des Hobbes hat ebenso wie das Symbol des Commonwealth seine Fähigkeit bewiesen, sich mit beliebigem geschichtlichen Inhalt zu füllen. Die politisch-religiöse Geschichte Europas hat die partikuläre Ekklesia zur

innerweltlich geschlossenen weiterentwickelt und auch die zu-
gehörigen Teufelsreiche hervorgebracht.

V.

DIE INNERWELTLICHE GEMEINSCHAFT

An den Grundzügen der europäischen politisch-religiösen
Symbolik hat sich seit dem 17. Jahrhundert nichts Wesentliches
mehr geändert. Hierarchie und Orden, universale und partikuläre Ekklesia, Gottesreich und Teufelsreich, Führertum und
Apokalypse bleiben die Formensprache der Gemeinschaftsreligion bis heute. Langsam wandeln sich dagegen die Inhalte
in der Richtung, die der Leviathan vorgezeichnet hat. Die
Ekklesia löst sich immer mehr aus dem Verband des univer-
salen Reiches mit der hierarchischen Spitze in Gott, bis sie sich
in einzelnen Fällen verselbständigt und innerweltlich schließt.
Sie ist nicht mehr sakral von der obersten Quelle her durch-
strömt, sondern ist selbst urspüngliche sakrale Substanz geworden. Reste der alten Gliederung bleiben noch in Formeln
ohne Tragweite erhalten, wie: daß die sakral geschlossene Gemeinschaft „im Auftrag Gottes" handle, wenn sie sich irdisch
ausbreitet; aber der „Auftrag Gottes" ist synonym mit innerweltlichen Formeln wie „Auftrag der Geschichte", „geschichtliche Sendung", „Befehl des Blutes" usw. Wir haben daher
nur noch früher gezogene Linien zu ergänzen und auf Sym-
ptome der neuen Inhaltserfüllung hinzuweisen, die als Fakten
jedermann bekannt sind, aber selten als Ausdrücke politischer
Religiosität verstanden werden.

Das gewaltige Fundament der neuen Innerweltlichkeit, an
dem die Jahrhunderte seit dem Spätmittelalter arbeiten, ist
die Kenntnis der Welt als Inventar von Seinstatsachen aller

Stufen und als Wissen um ihre Wesens- und Kausalzusammen-
hänge. Das Wissen vom Weltraum und der Natur, von der
Erde und den Völkern, die sie bewohnen, von ihrer Geschichte
und geistigen Differenzierung, von Pflanzen und Tieren, vom
Menschen als Leibwesen und als Geist, von seiner geschichtlichen Existenz und seiner Erkenntnisfähigkeit, seinem Seelenleben und seinen Trieben füllt massiv das neue Weltbild und
drängt alles Wissen um göttliche Ordnung an den Rand und
darüber hinaus. Die metaphysische Radikalfrage Schellings:
Warum ist etwas, warum ist nicht Nichts? — ist die Sorge
Weniger, breiten Massen bedeutet sie nichts für ihre religiöse
Haltung. Die Welt als Inhalt hat die Welt als Existenz verdrängt. Die Methoden der Wissenschaft als Formen der Er-
forschung des Weltinhaltes werden zu den allgemein verbind-
lichen, auf die sich die Haltung des Menschen zur Welt zu
gründen habe; seit dem 19. Jahrhundert wird über große
Perioden bis zur Gegenwart das Wort „metaphysisch" zum
Schimpfwort, Religion zu „Opium für das Volk" und in einer
neuen Wendung zu einer „Illusion" von fragwürdiger Zukunft.
Gegenformeln zu den Geistreligionen und ihrer Weltansicht
werden gebildet, die sich aus der Weltwissenschaft als der
gültigen Form der Einsicht im Gegensatz zu Offenbarung und
mystischem Denken legitimieren; es entstehen die „wissenschaftlichen Weltanschauungen", der „wissenschaftliche Sozia-
lismus", die „wissenschaftliche Rassenlehre", die „Welträtsel"
werden inventarisiert und gelöst. Gleichzeitig verfällt das
Wissen um die fundamentalen Seinsfragen und um die Formensprache, in der sie zu behandeln sind, als allgemeines und
zieht sich auf kleine Kreise zurück. Indifferentismus, Laizismus
und Atheismus werden die Merkmale des öffentlich-verbind-
lichen Weltbildes.

Die Menschen können den Weltinhalt so anwachsen lassen,
daß Welt und Gott hinter ihm verschwinden, aber sie können
nicht die Problematik ihrer Existenz aufheben. Sie lebt in

jeder Einzelseele weiter, und wenn Gott hinter der Welt unsichtbar geworden ist, dann werden die Inhalte der Welt zu neuen Göttern; wenn die Symbole der überweltlichen Religiosität verbannt werden, treten neue, aus der innerweltlichen Wissenschaftssprache entwickelte Symbole an ihre Stelle. Die innerweltliche Gemeinschaft hat ihre Apokalypse so wie die christliche Ekklesia, nur bestehen die neuen Apokalyptiker darauf, daß ihre Symbolschöpfungen wissenschaftliche Urteile seien. Wir haben schon von der joachitischen Symbolik einige Linien bis in die neuere Zeit gezogen, um auf das Kontinuum der Formensprache aufmerksam zu machen. Die innerweltliche Apokalypse braucht aus der joachitischen nur das überweltliche Endreich, den ewigen Sabbat, das Jenseits zu entfernen, um über die der Innerwelt angemessene Symbolsprache zu verfügen. Das Endreich ist nicht mehr eine überirdische Gemeinschaft des Geistes, sondern ein irdischer Zustand vollkommener Menschheit. Kants Ideen zu einer Geschichte in weltbürgerlicher Absicht entwerfen ein Geschichtsbild, in dem die menschliche Vernunftperson als innerweltliche zu immer höheren Stufen der Vollendung steigt, um schließlich unter geeigneten Führern bis zur zwangsfreien weltbürgerlichen Gemeinschaft fortzuschreiten. Die Menschheit ist das große Kollektivum, an dessen Entwicklung jeder Mensch zu seinem Teil mitzuarbeiten hat; sie ist irdisch geschlossen, nur als Ganzes schreitet sie fort, und der Sinn der Einzelexistenz ist das instrumentale Wirken zum kollektiven Fortschritt. Die Formel ist radikal kollektivistisch, so radikal, daß Kant gegenüber seiner eigenen Konstruktion das „Befremden" darüber ausdrückte, daß der Mensch von seiner Tätigkeit für das Kollektivum keinen Gewinn habe, sondern nur die späten Geschlechter in die Vollkommenheit des irdischen Paradieses eingehen werden. Die christlichen Widerstände regen sich, und Kant findet den Ausweg in die persönliche Unsterblichkeit, wenngleich sein Leser den Eindruck hat, daß sie ihm kein zu-

reichender Ersatz für das irdische Leben der vollkommenen
Vernunftperson zu sein schien. — Kants Offenbarung ist
menschheitlich — andere Apokalyptiker verengen ihre Symbolik auf die Sendung einer partikulären Gemeinschaft. Fichte
entwickelt seine Offenbarung im Zusammenhang mit der Symbolik des Johannesevangeliums; das Endreich, als irdisches,
ist das Reich Gottes, und kein anderes Volk ist befähigt, die
Menschheit zu regenerieren und das Gottesreich herbeizufüh-
ren, als das Urvolk der Deutschen. Comte entwickelt die Theo-
rien Vicos und Saint-Simons zu dem Gesetz der drei weltgeschichtlichen Stadien, des religiösen, des metaphysischen und
des heraufziehenden positiv-wissenschaftlichen, und findet, daß
die Franzosen die Träger des positiven Geistes sind. Marx
gliedert die Geschichte in die urkommunistische, die klassen-
staatliche und die endkommunistische und erkennt als Träger
der Entwicklung zum Endreich das Proletariat. Rassentheoreti-
ker verstehen seit Gobineau die Weltgeschichte als Bewegung
und Kampf der Rassen und sehen als Träger eine auserwählte
nordische oder germanische. — Jede der Apokalypsen hat in
der europäischen Geschichte auch ihre Teufelssymbolik geschaffen. Von der katholischen Kirche als dem Satan, der zum
Leviathan gehört, wurde schon gesprochen. Kants Teufel ist
die menschliche Triebhaftigkeit; Fichte hat gigantisch die Figur
des Satans Napoleon entworfen; zur positivistischen Apokalypse gehören Religion und Metaphysik als das Böse; zum
Proletariat der Bourgeois; zur auserwählten Rasse die minderwertige, vor allem die Juden als „Gegenrasse".
Der gemeinsame Zug der neuen Symbolik ist ihr „Wissen-
schafts"-Charakter. Von ihm geht eine eigentümliche Dynamik
aus, die im Verlauf von weniger als einem Jahrhundert die
seelische Struktur der innerweltlichen Gemeinschaft stark verändert hat. Die Apokalypsen, die wir eben aufzählten, sind
„naiv", d. h. sie nehmen für ihre Thesen gutgläubig den Charakter wissenschaftlicher Urteile in Anspruch. Seit der Mitte

des 19. Jahrhunderts beginnt, ausgehend vom Marxismus, eine immer radikaler werdende Kritik der Apokalypsen unter dem Titel der Enthüllung von Ideologien. Die Enthüller wollen nachweisen, daß die symbolischen Systeme den Forderungen wissenschaftlicher Methodik nicht entsprechen und daß sie aus bestimmten Interessenlagen geformt wurden. Mit dem Wissenschaftsanspruch stellt sich die Apokalypse auf den Boden wissenschaftlicher Diskussion und wird von ihren eigenen Voraussetzungen her aufgelöst. Man könnte nun glauben, daß als Folge der wechselseitigen ideologiekritischen Zersetzung sich die Rückkehr zu kritikfesteren Weltbildern anbahnen würde — aber es geschieht das Merkwürdige: die Haltung der innerweltlichen Religiosität ist so stark, daß nicht ihre Apokalypsen unter dem Angriff wissenschaftlicher Kritik zerfallen, sondern daß der Wahrheitsbegriff umgebildet wird. In der ersten Phase dieser Entwicklung wird der nichtwissenschaftliche Charakter der Symbole anerkannt; der politischreligiöse Mensch läßt sie aber darum nicht fallen, vielmehr wird mit Rücksicht auf den massenbindenden Wert das Symbol gehalten, auch wenn es wissenschaftlich nicht zureicht. An die Stelle der naiven Apokalypse tritt die bewußte, an die Stelle des Systems, das sich als vernunfttheoretisches, nationalökonomisches oder soziologisches gibt, der „Mythus"; der Mythus wird bewußt erzeugt, um Massen affektuell zu binden und in politisch wirksame Zustände der Heilserwartung zu versetzen. Da der Mythus sich nicht durch überweltliche Offenbarung legitimieren und der wissenschaftlichen Kritik nicht standhalten kann, entwickelt sich in einer zweiten Phase ein neuer Wahrheitsbegriff, der Begriff der von Rosenberg sogenannten organischen Wahrheit. Wir finden die Ansätze schon bei Hobbes in der These, daß eine Lehre, welche Einheit und Frieden des Commonwealth stört, nicht wahr sein könne; die Theorie wird jetzt weiter gebildet zu der Auffassung, daß wahr sei, was das Dasein der organisch geschlossenen innerweltlichen Volksgemeinschaft fördere. Erkenntnis und Kunst, Mythus und Sitte sind wahr, wenn sie im Dienste des rassegebundenen Volkstums stehen. „Von da kommen sie her, da gehen sie wieder hin. Und ihr entscheidendes Kriterium finden sie alle daran, ob sie Gestalt und inneren Wert dieses Rassevolkstums steigern, es wertmäßiger ausbilden, es lebenskräftiger gestalten oder nicht." Die Mythenbildung wird damit der rationalen Diskussion entzogen und nähert sich der eigentlichen Symbolik als einem Reich von sinnlichen Gestalten, in denen innerweltliche Erfahrung und transzendentes Erlebnis sich zu faßbarer Einheit verbinden.

Der pragmatische Zug der innerweltlichen Glaubenshaltung hat zur Folge, daß der Mensch dieses religiösen Typus bereit ist, die psychologische Technik der Mythenerzeugung, -propaganda und sozialen Durchsetzung zu kennen, sich aber durch dieses Wissen nicht in seinem Glauben stören zu lassen. Wenn das, was die Gemeinschaft fördert, wahr ist, dann sind auch die Mittel, die den gemeinschaftsfördernden Mythus durchsetzen, nicht nur die richtigen im technischen Sinn, sondern auch die erlaubten und sogar gebotenen im gemeinschaftsreligiösen Sinn. Es ist daher möglich gewesen, die Technik der Mythenpropaganda auf den hohen gegenwärtigen Stand zu entwickeln, ohne daß das Faktum der Propaganda ihren Zweck selbst zerstört. Die Einsichten der Tiefenpsychologie in das Triebleben des einzelnen und der Massen konnten technisch verwertet werden, ohne daß der Appell an die Triebhaftigkeit Widerstände hervorgerufen hätte. Die Einsicht in die Triebuntergründe hat ebensowenig zu einer Rationalisierung der Persönlichkeit geführt wie die Ideologiekritik zur Zerstörung des innerweltlichen Offenbarungsglaubens, sondern im Gegenteil zu der Anerkennung, daß der Haß stärker sei als die Liebe, und daß darum die Enthemmung der Angriffstriebe und der Aufbau der Haßeinstellung die gebotenen Mittel zur Verwirklichung der Gemeinschaftsziele seien.

Dieses wichtige Phänomen wird in seiner Tragweite als Merkmal der innerweltlichen Religiosität deutlicher, wenn wir es mit einer überweltlichen Zweckmittelbetrachtung wie der des Ignatius von Loyola vergleichen. Die Betrachtungen des Ignatius erstrecken sich auf die Zuordnung der richtigen Mittel für das eine Ziel der Kreatur, der Ehre Gottes und dem Heil der Seele zu leben. Zu diesem Ziel müssen die zweckdienlichen Mittel gewählt werden, „so daß ich nicht das Ziel dem Mittel unterordne und gewaltsam unterstelle, sondern das Mittel dem Ziele". Im klaren Bewußtsein von der menschlichen Triebhaftigkeit wird die sorgfältige Prüfung empfohlen, ob irgend eine Form der Lebensführung nicht „ungeordneten Neigungen" entsprechen und darum gewählt würde, in der Hoffnung, daß Gott der Seele trotzdem entgegenkommen werde, anstatt die Lebensführung als Mittel völlig dem Zweck des Seelenheiles und der Gottesehrung unterzuordnen. Die Lebensführung hat also die Stelle eines irdischen Mittels, das seine Bedeutung von dem überweltlichen Ziel her empfängt und nichts enthalten darf, was mit dem heiligen Zweck unverträglich ist. Wenn an die Stelle Gottes die innerweltliche Kollektivexistenz rückt, wird die Person zum dienenden Glied des sakralen Weltinhaltes; sie wird Instrument, wie Kant schon — und noch — mit „Befremden" bemerkte; das Problem ihrer Lebensführung, ihrer physischen und geistigen Existenz ist nur wichtig im Zusammenhang der Existenz der umfassenden Gemeinschaft als des Realissimum. In der Haltung innerweltlicher Religiosität akzeptiert der Mensch diese Stellung; er nimmt sich selbst als Werkzeug, als Hegelschen Maschinenteil des großen Ganzen, und unterwirft sich willig den technischen Mitteln, mit denen die Organisation des Kollektivums ihn eingliedert. Das Wissen um die Weltinhalte und die darauf begründete Technik sind nicht die temporal untergeordneten Mittel für das ewige Ziel des Lebens im überweltlichen Gott, sondern das Lebensblut des innerweltlichen

Gottes selbst; sie bauen das corpus mysticum des Kollektivums und verbinden die Glieder zu der Einheit des Leibes; sie werden nicht als Verbrechen gegen die Würde der Person verworfen, sie werden nicht einmal nur ertragen aus der Einsicht in ein Gebot des Augenblicks, sie werden gefordert und ersehnt als Methoden religiös-ekstatischer Verbindung des Menschen mit seinem Gott. Die Erzeugung des Mythus und seine Propaganda durch Zeitung und Rundfunk, die Reden und Gemeinschaftsfeiern, die Versammlungen und das Marschieren, die Planarbeit und das Sterben im Kampf sind die innerweltlichen Formen der unio mystica.

SYMBOLIK

Die Symbolik der vollständig geschlossenen innerweltlichen Ekklesia brauchte über das Leviathansymbol nur wenig hinauszugehen — der entscheidende Schritt war die Dekapitierung Gottes. In der Symbolik des Hobbes schloß sich die Vielzahl der Menschen zu der Einheit des Commonwealth nach den Regeln gottgewollten Rechtes zusammen; und das christliche Commonwealth unterstand als Kollektivperson Gott mit dem Souverän als Gottesmittler. Auf die Verwandtschaft mit der Reichsreligion des Echnaton und die Orientierung des Symbols am abrahamitischen Gottesvolk wurde schon hingewiesen. In der vollendet innerweltlichen Symbolik wird nun die Verbindung zu Gott durchschnitten, und an seine Stelle tritt als Legitimierungsquelle der Gemeinschaftsperson die Gemeinschaft selbst. Die Sprache der Symbolik ist ziemlich gut rational entwickelt und auch verhältnismäßig uniform, weil die Theoretiker der zwei radikal innerweltlichen Ekklesiae, der faschistisch-italienischen und der nationalsozialistisch-deutschen, aus dem gemeinsamen Wortschatz der deutschen Ro-

mantik schöpfen. Die sakrale Substanz ist für beide der Volksgeist oder der objektive Geist, ein durch die Zeit dauerndes
Realissimum, das in den einzelnen Menschen als Gliedern
ihres Volkes und ihren Werken geschichtliche Wirklichkeit
wird. Mussolini spricht vom Faschismus als einer religiösen
Idee und von der Politik des Regimes als religiöser Politik,
weil der Faschismus von der Annahme ausgehe, daß der
Mensch mit einer Volontà obiettiva in Verbindung stehe und
durch diese Verbindung Persönlichkeit in einem geistigen
Reich, im Reich seines Volkes, gewinne.

Auf dem Grunde dieser Annahme erhebt sich der Bau der
Symbolik in den Formen, die Hobbes durchgebildet hat. Das
Volk ist das „Volk der Vielheit" als Gemeinschaft von Sprache,
Brauchtum, Kultur, wirtschaftlichem Handeln, und es wird
zum „Volk der Einheit", zur geschichtlichen Person, durch die
politische Organisation. An die Stelle der Vertragshypothese
des Hobbes und der Wahl des Souveräns tritt ein anderes,
innerweltlich-sakrales Ausleseprinzip für die Persönlichkeitsträger der Gemeinschaft: In der italienischen wie in der deutschen Theorie steht die Person des Volksgenossen zwar in Beziehung zum Volksgeist, denn nur durch diese Beziehung hat
der Volksgenosse Status im Volk als einem spirituellen Körper — aber der Status ist nicht gleich für alle. In manchen
Menschen, in den wenigen, lebt der Volksgeist stärker, in
anderen, den vielen, lebt er schwächer, und nur in einem
drückt er sich vollkommen aus, im Führer. „Der Führer ist
von der Idee durchdrungen; sie handelt durch ihn. Aber er
ist es auch, der dieser Idee die lebendige Form zu geben vermag. In ihm verwirklicht sich der Volksgeist und bildet sich der
Volkswille; in ihm gewinnt das geschlechterumspannende und
deshalb niemals in seiner Ganzheit konkret versammelte Volk
die sichtbare Gestalt. Er ist der Repräsentant des Volkes" —
schreibt ein deutscher Theoretiker. Der Führer ist die Stelle,
an der der Volksgeist in die geschichtliche Realität einbricht;

zum Führer spricht der innerweltliche Gott wie der überweltliche zu Abraham, und der Führer formt die Gottesworte um
zum Befehl an die engere Gefolgschaft und an das Volk. Die
Berührung mit der Symbolik des Leviathan ist so eng, daß sogar die gleichen Worte verwendet werden, um die mystische
Personifikation der Ekklesia zu fassen: der Führer ist in der
deutschen Theorie der „Repräsentant" im gleichen Sinne, wie
der Souverän des Hobbes der Repräsentant, der Persönlichkeitsträger des Commonwealth ist. Ein gewisser Unterschied
besteht an diesem Punkt zwischen der italienischen und der
deutschen Symbolik insofern, als der italienische Volksgeist
mehr spirituell verstanden wird, während in der deutschen der
Geist blutgebunden ist und der Führer zum Sprecher des
Volksgeistes und Repräsentanten des Volkes kraft seiner
rassenmäßigen Einheit mit dem Volk wird.
Ein weiteres Glied der Theorie ist nicht ebenso sorgfältig
durchrationalisiert wie die bisherigen: der schwierige Punkt ist
der Persönlichkeitsstatus der Volksgenossen. Sie sind einerseits
Glieder des Volkes, weil der Volksgeist in ihnen lebt, anderseits stehen sie mit dem Volksgeist politisch-organisatorisch
durch die Vermittlung des Führers in Verbindung. Die Reichsreligion des Echnaton hat das Problem radikal gelöst, indem
sie dem Pharao die Mittlerfunktion gab und den Willen des
Gottes von ihm zum Volk herabsteigen ließ. In der innerweltlichen Symbolik sind Führer und Volk gemeinsam verbunden
in der sakralen Substanz, die im einen wie im andern lebt; der
Gott steht nicht außerhalb, sondern lebt in den Menschen
selbst; und es wäre daher möglich, daß der Volksgeist sich auch
im Willen des Volkes äußert, daß die Volkesstimme zur
Gottesstimme wird. Die Theoretiker bewältigen das Problem,
indem sie einerseits den geschichtlichen Bestand des Volkes als
Äußerung des Volksgeistes in Brauchtum und Sitte, Sprache
und Kultur anerkennen und — besonders in der deutschen
Theorie — die Staatsorganisation als Bau deuten, in dessen

Schutz das Volkstum sich artgemäß entfalten kann; anderseits lehnen sie die politische Willensbestimmung durch das Volk ab — wieder besonders deutlich in der deutschen Theorie: der Führer ist der einzige Willensträger des Volkes. In der Lehre von der Volksabstimmung wird mit aller Entschiedenheit der Gedanke zurückgewiesen, daß der Abstimmungsakt ein Willensakt des Volkes sei. Die Abstimmung soll die Übereinstimmung zwischen dem im Führer verkörperten objektiven Volkswillen und der subjektiven Überzeugung der Volksangehörigen nach außen zeigen und bekräftigen; die Volksabstimmung ist Bekenntnis zum Führer, nicht Kundgabe eines eigenen Willens. Wenn daher die Abstimmung den Führerwillen nicht bestätigt, braucht der Führer nicht vor dem Volkswillen zurückzuweichen, denn die Versagung ist nicht objektiver Wille des Volkes, sondern Ausdruck einer subjektiven Willkür. Nach dieser Konstruktion nähert sich die Symbolik sehr stark der ägyptischen; nur zum Führer spricht der Gott, das Volk erfährt seinen Willen nur durch die Vermittlung des Führers.

GLAUBE

Die Welt der Symbole ist ein Fertiges, ein Letztes — wir wollen hinabsteigen zu den Ursprüngen, zu den Kräften, welche die symbolischen Formen schaffen. Gerhard Schumanns „Lieder vom Reich" sind einer der stärksten Ausdrücke politisch-religiöser Erregungen. Sie machen es möglich, den Seelenbewegungen nachzugehen, aus deren Stoff sich die Symbole und die geschichtliche Wirklichkeit der innerweltlichen Gemeinschaft aufbauen. Sie haben als religiöse Erregungen ihre Wurzeln im Erlebnis der Kreatürlichkeit; aber das Realissimum, in dem sie sich erlösen, ist nicht, wie im christlichen Erlebnis, Gott, sondern das Volk und die Bruderschaft der verschworenen Gefährten, und die Ekstasen sind nicht geistig, son-

dern triebhaft, und münden im Blutrausch der Tat. Wir geben
die Formeln wieder, in denen der Dichter selbst sein Erlebnis
ausspricht.

Die Grunderregung der kreatürlichen Verlassenheit wird
beschrieben als Zustand traumhafter Unwirklichkeit, der Kälte,
sich verschließender Einsamkeit; aus ihm bricht die Seele
brennend aus, um sich dem heiligen Ganzen zu vereinen;
ein heißer Strom der Erregung reißt sie mit sich aus ihrer
Vereinzelung in die Bruderschaft von „Erde, Licht und Ding".
Der Übergang aus der Haltung starren Stolzes in das Schmel-
zen und Strömen ist aktiv und passiv zugleich; die Seele will
und erlebt sich selbst als tätig im Durchbrechen von Wider-
ständen, und sie ist zugleich getrieben, mitgerissen von einem
Strom, dem sie sich nur hingeben muß.

Die Seele hat sich mit dem Strom brüderlichen Weltfließens
vereinigt: „Und ich war Einer. Und das Ganze floß." Der
Strom trägt weiter, durchstößt alle Wandungen und läßt die
Seele einmünden in das Ganze des Volkes; im Finden und in
der Vereinigung entpersönlicht sich die Seele; sie befreit sich
völlig von dem kalten Ring ihres Selbst; sie erweitert sich über
ihre frierende Kleinheit hinaus, wird „gut und groß"; im Verlieren ihres Selbst steigt sie auf in die größere Realität des
Volkes: „Verlor mich selbst und fand das Volk, das Reich."
In einer weiteren Vision verjüngt sich die deutsche Erde, ein
neuer Himmel wölbt sich über ihr, und aus dem Chaos steigt
der Gral, das Bild der neuen Ordnung, dessen Dienst sich die
Seele mit Gefährten in einer Schwurbrüderschaft verpflichtet.
Die Wirklichkeit aber ist noch drückend, schwer lastet die Zeit
auf dem Reich, und die „Strengen" wenden sich ab, magisch
gebannt durch ihren Schwur, „der Flammenstunde harrend,
die sie meinten". — Schwüler drückt die Not, das Leben stockt,
bis aus der Glut des letzten Augenblicks vor dem Zusammen-
bruch aus Tausenden der Schrei bricht: „Den Führer! Knechte
uns! Herr, mach uns frei!"

In einer Ölbergvision — „Da kam die Nacht. Der Eine
stand und rang" — nimmt der ersehnte Führer den Befehl
Gottes an, sein Volk zu erlösen:

> „ ... Und niedersteigend
> Trug er die Fackel in die Nacht hinein.

> Die Millionen beugten sich ihm schweigend.
> Erlöst. Der Himmel flammte morgenbleich.
> Die Sonne wuchs. Und mit ihr wuchs das Reich."

Auch die letzte Vision überschreitet nicht den Raum der
religiösen Erregung der Einzelseele. Die Not des Volkes und
die Erlösung durch den Führer sind nicht äußere geschichtliche
Ereignisse, die der Sprecher als Dichter zum Bild formt; die
Not ist die Not der Seele, die sich ekstatisch im Volk verloren
hat, sein Leid ist ihr Leid; und der Führer, der nach dem
Ringen mit Gott als Heiland vom Berg herabsteigt, um das
Volk zu erlösen, erlöst die Einzelseele, die sich dem Dienst
am Gral, dem Bau am Dom des Reiches, verschworen hat.
Die religiöse Erregung beruhigt sich nicht in der Vereinigung mit dem Ganzen; sie braucht die Spannung des Kampfes
und die Ekstase der Tat. Die Erlösungstat des Führers und
der Sieg des Bundes der verschworenen „Strengen" in der
empirischen Reichsgründung zieht einen Schnitt, nach dem sich
unzweideutig ausspricht, was vorher schon zu hören war: daß
das persönliche religiöse Drama und das Drama des gesamten
Volkes auseinanderfallen können. In der Zeit der Spannung
und des Harrens sind die Gralsdiener die Träger und Vor-
kämpfer des kommenden Reiches; nach der politisch-organisa-
torischen Etablierung spaltet sich die Inbrunst der Strengen
vom Alltag der kampfentspannten Geschäfte und Geschäftig-
keit. In dem Gedicht: „Und nach den Siegen kommen, die sie
feiern. — Dann sind sie groß, und der Soldat ist stumm" —

wendet sich der Dichter gegen die flach und ahnungslos Geschäftigen, die den Sinn des Geschehenen erklären wollen, während die Kämpfer das Schicksal schauernd nach den neuen Befehlen fragen; sie sind weiter die Getriebenen zu neuem Kampf: „Da ist nicht Zeit, in Festen hinzudämmern. — Wir sind daran, das Neue Reich zu hämmern"; während die anderen nicht fassen „Das Schicksal, das anhebt, sich zu vollenden". Ein Gebet steigt:

„Laß es nicht zu, daß ich mich häuslich einrichte.
Laß es nicht zu, daß ich satt werde und zur Ruhe mahne.
Stoß mich in jede Verzweiflung und Unruhe des Herzens."

Ein anderer Vers mahnt: „Wirf dich noch über dein Wollen! — Über die Sterne! Hinauf!" — Der Wille, sich selbst zu verlieren und ekstatisch auszubrechen, wird getrieben von tief-erregender Existenzangst, wie im Münstergedicht:

„Und alle Angst, das fürchterliche Schauern
Bricht auf: von Turm zu Turm empor empor!"

Das Gedicht „Die Tat" zeigt die Stufen der Taterregung bis zur Entspannung. Nicht der Sieg ist der Sinn der Tat, sondern die Tat selbst; der Schmerz, der dem Feind zugefügt wird, soll in die Seele des Täters zurückfahren: „Und wenn du schlägst, triff in dein eigen Herz"; der Freund muß vernichtet werden wie der Feind, bis zur völligen Vereinsamung; in der Tat, der bösen, vernichtenden Tat, schlägt der Täter sich selbst bis zum Auslöschen des eigenen Wünschens und Wollens; die nackte, ziellose Tat, das Sichverbeißen und Zerfleischen sind Akte mystischer Selbstauflösung und der Kommunion mit der Welt bis zur Entspannung im Blutrausch: „Die Tat war gut, wenn du sie rot geblutet."
Für diese Täter, die Gezeichneten, ist die neue Welt des

Sieges dumpf und schal; im Alltag sind sie heimatlos und bei
den Feiern fühlen sie sich fremd:

„In harten Blicken und in ungerührten
Tragen sie nur Schafotte, keine Gnade."

Gelähmt, dumpf, manchmal sich bäumend, warten sie,
„lauernd auf Befehl". Sie finden sich wieder aus dem Getriebe
als „ein Haufe von Entschloßnen", verbunden unter sich,
„weil Herzblut Männerherzen zu sich reißt", der Kern, die
Seele des Reiches, ergeben nur „dem Führer, welcher einsam
ist", dem Führer, von dem sie nachts träumen.

„Aus ihren Schritten hallt das Blutgericht.
In ihrer Seele tragen sie den Gral.
Knechte des Führers, Hüter und Rächer zugleich.
In ihnen brennt, mit ihnen wächst das Reich."

VI.

EPILOG

Wir haben uns um die politischen Religionen als Erken-
nende bemüht — ziehen wir darum zuerst das Fazit der Erkenntnis: Das Leben der Menschen in politischer Gemeinschaft
kann nicht als ein profaner Bezirk abgegrenzt werden, in dem
wir es nur mit Fragen der Rechts- und Machtorganisation zu
tun haben. Die Gemeinschaft ist auch ein Bereich religiöser
Ordnung, und die Erkenntnis eines politischen Zustandes ist
in einem entscheidenden Punkt unvollständig, wenn sie nicht
die religiösen Kräfte der Gemeinschaft und die Symbole, in

denen sie Ausdruck finden, mitumfaßt, oder sie zwar umfaßt, aber nicht als solche erkennt, sondern in a-religiöse Kategorien übersetzt. In der politischen Gemeinschaft lebt der Mensch mit allen Zügen seines Wesens von den leiblichen bis zu den geistigen und religiösen. Wir haben die Beispiele zur Verdeutlichung nur dem mediterranen und westeuropäischen Kulturkreis entnommen, aber die These will allgemein sein und gilt ebenso für die politischen Formen des Ostens. Immer ist die politische Gemeinschaft in den Zusammenhang des Welt- und Gotterlebens der Menschen eingegliedert, sei es, daß der politische Bereich in der Hierarchie des Seins eine untere Stufe der göttlichen Ordnung einnimmt, sei es, daß er selbst vergöttlicht wird. Immer ist auch die Sprache der Politik durchweht von Erregungen der Religiosität und wird dadurch zur Symbolik in dem prägnanten Sinn der Durchdringung der weltinhaltlichen mit transzendent-göttlicher Erfahrung. In jeder der Hochkulturen sind Elemente der symbolischen Formensprache wiederzufinden, die wir an den mediterran-europäischen Beispielen entwickelt haben: die Hierarchie, in der die sakrale Substanz vom überweltlichen Gott zur Gemeinschaft der Kreaturen sich ausbreitet; die Ekklesia als sakrale Gemeinschaftssubstanz; die Apokalypse als Offenbarung des Reiches; die heiligen Könige als Gottesmittler und Persönlichkeitsträger der Gemeinschaft.

Treten wir nun in den religiösen Bereich selbst ein — so ist die christliche Entscheidung klar; der Frankfurter sagt in der Deutschen Theologie: „Wenn die Kreatur etwas Gutes sich selbst zumißt, wie Wesen, Leben, Wissen, Erkenntnis, Können, kurzum all das, was man gut nennen muß, so als ob sie das sei oder habe, als ob es ihr zugehöre oder aus ihr komme, so kehrt sie sich ab. Was tat der Teufel anders? Was anders war bei ihm Fall und Abkehr, als daß er sich anmaßte, er wär auch etwas, und ein Wer sein und ein Eigen haben wollte. Dieses Annehmen und sein ,Ich' und ,Mich', sein ,Mir' und ,Mein', das war sein Abkehren und sein Fall. Und so ist er noch." Es ist nicht gleichgültig, wie der Bereich menschlich-politischer Organisation in die Seinsordnung eingegliedert wird. Die innerweltliche Religiosität, die das Kollektivum, sei es die Menschheit, das Volk, die Klasse, die Rasse, oder den Staat, als Realissimum erlebt, ist Abfall von Gott; und manche christliche Denker lehnen es darum ab, die innerweltliche politische Religion mit der Geistreligion des Christentums auch nur sprachlich auf eine Stufe zu stellen; sie sprechen von Dämonologien im Gegensatz zum Gottesglauben, oder von einem Glauben, der Menschenwerk ist, einer „mystique humaine", zum Unterschied vom wahren Glauben. Der Glaube an den Menschen als Quelle des Guten und der Verbesserung der Welt, wie er die Aufklärung beherrscht, und der Glaube an das Kollektivum als geheimnisvoll göttliche Substanz, wie er sich seit dem 19. Jahrhundert ausbreitet, ist antichristlich in der Sprache des Frankfurters, ist Abkehr. — Und im Sinne der undogmatischen vita contemplativa, der Schau des Seins im Reichtum des Stufenbaues von der Natur bis zu Gott, verdeckt die innerweltliche Religiosität und ihre Symbolik die wesentlichsten Teile der Wirklichkeit; sie versperrt den Weg zur Realität Gottes und verzerrt die Verhältnisse der untergöttlichen Seinsstufen.

Weder die Erkenntnis aber, noch die christliche Entscheidung löst das Mysterium Gottes und des Seins. Die Gottesschöpfung enthält das Böse, die Seinsherrlichkeit wird getrübt vom Elend der Kreatur, die Ordnung der Gemeinschaft wird mit Haß und Blut, mit Jammer und im Abfall von Gott gebaut. Der Schellingschen Weltgrundfrage „Warum ist Etwas, warum ist nicht Nichts?" folgt die andere: „Warum ist es so, wie es ist?" — die Frage der Theodizee.

Quellennotiz.

Der historisch-tatsächliche Inhalt des vorliegenden Essays stützt sich fast ohne Ausnahme auf die Quellen selbst.

Die theoretischen Annahmen und geschichtlichen Deutungen sind nicht neuartig, sondern geben den gegenwärtigen Stand der Wissenschaft wieder. Für den Leser, der sich um das Verständnis von Einzelfragen weiter bemühen will, seien einige der Hauptwerke angeführt, welche die berührten Probleme betreffen.

Die religionswissenschaftlichen Annahmen folgen im allgemeinen Erich P r z y w a r a, S. J., Religionsphilosophie katholischer Theologie (Handbuch der Philosophie. Herausgegeben von A. Bäumler und M. Schröter. Abteilung II. Natur-Geist-Gott). Verlag R. Oldenbourg. München und Berlin. 1927.

Eine Fundgrube für Erscheinungen der neuen Massenreligiosität am Ausgang des 19. Jahrhunderts ist das Werk von William J a m e s, The Varieties of Religions Experience. A Study in Human Nature. Longmans, Green & Co. London 1902.

Für die Erkenntnis gegenwärtiger politisch-religiöser Erscheinungen ist wichtig die Abhandlung von Etienne de G r e e f f, Le drame humain et la psychologie des „mystiques" humaines (enthalten in Foi et „Mystiques" Humaines. Etudes Carmélitaines. 22 Année. Vol. I. Avril 1937).

Die philosophisch-anthropologischen Grundansichten des Verfassers stützen sich auf die breite gegenwärtige Literatur zu diesem Gegenstand; leicht zugänglich ist das Werk von Max S c h e l e r, Die Stellung des Menschen im Kosmos. Otto Reichl Verlag. Darmstadt. 1928.

Das Kapitel über Echnaton stützt sich auf. J. H. B r e a s t e d, Geschichte Ägyptens. 2. Auflage. Phaidon-Verlag. Wien. 1936.

Zu den Fragen des europäischen Mittelalters, im besonderen zum Problem des Joachim von Floris, siehe Alois D e m p f, Sacrum Imperium, Geschichts- und Staatsphilosophie des Mittelalters und der politischen Renaissance. Verlag von R. Oldenbourg. München und Berlin. 1929.

Über die Probleme des 12. und 13. Jahrhunderts ferner das Werk von Georges d e L a g a r d e, La Naissance de l'Esprit laïque au déclin du Moyen-Age. I. und II. Editions Béatrice. 1934.

Ferner Ernst K a n t o r o w i c z, Kaiser Friedrich der Zweite. Georg
Bondi. Berlin. 1928.

An prinzipiellen neueren Versuchen, das politische Problem als religiö-
ses zu verstehen, ist dem Verfasser ein einziger bekannt geworden: Alexander U l a r, Die Politik. Untersuchung über die völkerpsychologischen Bedingungen gesellschaftlicher Organisation. Rütten und Loening. Frankfurt
a. M. 1906. (Die Gesellschaft. Sammlung sozialpsychologischer Monographien. Herausgegeben von Martin Buber. Band 3.)

TORONTO STUDIES IN THEOLOGY